Unashamed

Published by Barbour Books, an imprint of Barbour Publishing, Inc., 1810 Barbour Drive, Uhrichsville, Ohio 44683, www.barbourbooks.com.

Our mission is to inspire the world with the life-changing message of the Bible.

ecpa Member of the
Evangelical Christian
Publishers Association

Printed in China.

Unashamed

Devotions & Prayers
for a Burden-Free Heart

Janice Thompson

BARBOUR BOOKS
An Imprint of Barbour Publishing, Inc.

Shame Off You!

"Shame on you! You should be ashamed of yourself!"

How many times did you hear these words spoken over you when you were growing up? Maybe hundreds. Most parents, friends, or loved ones don't even realize what they're saying when those words come spilling out, but shame has sticking power.

With every naughty deed, every poor report card, every disobedient act, shame strikes to the core. And it's difficult to part with once it has weaseled its way into your story. With every critique about weight, every harsh word about academic disappointments, every "You're not as pretty as your sister," shame wraps you in its tentacles and squeezes a bit harder until you begin to wonder how you will ever break free.

We were never meant to carry shame. This ominous cloud was never part of God's plan for His kids. No matter what was spoken over you, no matter how many times you were criticized, you have nothing to be ashamed of. If you're walking in relationship with Christ, if you've accepted His free gift of salvation, then the shame is *off* you and on Him. He bore it all on the cross, once and for all, so that you could be set free.

As you read through these devotions, be encouraged. Allow God to cut the cords that have bound you to shame. Step out in freedom and learn to guard the words that you speak over others as you walk a new journey, free in Him.

Freedom!

*Now the Lord is the Spirit, and where
the Spirit of the Lord is, there is freedom.*
2 CORINTHIANS 3:17

. . . .

Picture a prisoner on release day. He has spent years in a dark, dank cell, shrouded in hopelessness. Nothing about his confined situation has prepared him for life on the outside. But he dares to hope, dares to dream that he will leave his past behind and step into new life beyond those foreboding walls, a life unlike anything he has experienced thus far.

The gate swings wide, and he steps through, his heart beating fast. Does he really deserve freedom after the life he's lived, the things he's done? Will others always cast shame and blame, or will he really get the second chance he's been longing for?

Beams of sunlight blind him, and he squints to see the street, where a car is waiting to pick him up. With new resolve, he steps toward his new life, free from the past. No looking back. No memories of what sent him to prison in the first place. Hope abounds, and he sheds one mentality to embrace another.

So many of us can relate to this story. We've been bound by years of sin and shame, living in confined spaces. The notion that freedom is possible seems ludicrous at best. There's no way out for us, or so we've led ourselves to believe.

In many ways, we are like the woman we read about in the Gospel of John, the one caught in the act of adultery. She was living in a prison that seemed impossible to escape, a lifestyle that kept her wound tighter than a spool of thread. But Jesus looked upon her with mercy and grace. He didn't holler, "Aren't you ashamed of yourself?" or "Shame on you!" No, He left that to the Pharisees. Instead, He bent down, wrote a few words in the dirt, and pricked the hearts of her accusers with these words: "Let him who is without sin among you be the first to throw a stone at her" (John 8:7).

Maybe there have been a few stone throwers in your life. Maybe they've contributed to the dark cloud of shame hovering over you. Today is your day to step out from under that cloud, to look beyond the prison walls. Allow God to bring complete healing—be set free from the shame, but also take the time to forgive the ones who cloaked you in it. When you let go of the shame and bitterness, you'll walk into the sunlight, never looking back.

Father, I want to be set free. For all who wounded me,
I offer forgiveness. For those who spoke shame over me,
I step out from under their words. I'm not content to
live in confinement anymore, Lord. Right here,
right now, I proclaim my freedom. Amen.

Misplaced Shame

The Lord is a stronghold for the oppressed,
a stronghold in times of trouble.
PSALM 9:9

She was never meant to be the recipient of the shame, yet she wore it like a badge. The shame belonged to another, one who had his way with her when she was just a child. His sin, his crime, should have resulted in his shame, not hers. And yet she couldn't seem to break free from the burden of guilt.

She never knew what hit her. Instead of admitting his wrong, her perpetrator pressed the shame onto her, insisting she was somehow to blame for his wicked choices. How he managed to pull it off, she never could understand.

And she never fought that allegation. Broken, confused, and terrified, she did her best just to survive. On she went through the years, carrying a burden that should have landed squarely on the shoulders of the one who had wronged her so cruelly. But she couldn't figure out how to rid herself of it, no matter how hard she tried. Would she remain bound for the rest of her life, or could someone finally set her free?

Maybe you know this woman. Maybe you *are* this woman. The misplaced shame she carried was never hers in the first place, yet she lived with it for years. Only the power of Christ can both break bondages and change perceptions and thought patterns.

What about you? Have you carried misplaced shame as a result of crimes perpetrated against you as a child or an adult? Are you still wounded and broken over acts that were done to you or done against you, things you did not cause? Today God longs for you to be set free from the pain and shame of the past. Start by acknowledging that shame has no place in your story. Then begin to see yourself walking in freedom. Ask God to radically transform your thoughts so that you can be set free once and for all.

Father, please change my thinking! I don't want to carry this burden any longer. I forgive the one who wounded me. I step away from that situation, both mentally and physically. Today I lift this false shame I've carried and place it into Your capable hands, to be done away with for good. Thank You for the freedom only You can bring. Amen.

The New Has Come

Therefore, if anyone is in Christ, he is a new creation.
The old has passed away; behold, the new has come.

2 CORINTHIANS 5:17

- -

With a bleak past as an ex-convict, fictional character Jean Valjean (from *Les Misérables*) feels he has nowhere to turn. He is a lost soul and wonders if he will ever gain any semblance of normalcy again.

A local bishop agrees to take him in for the night. Out of desperation, Valjean makes a monumental decision that will alter his life in a variety of ways: he steals valuable silverware from the precious, godly man who gave him shelter. When the police arrive, Valjean's story takes an amazing twist. Instead of accusing him, the bishop covers for Valjean. He protects him. After the police leave, the bishop makes Valjean promise that he will turn his life around.

And turn his life around he does. Valjean goes on to reinvent himself as both mayor and prominent factory owner. He spends much of the rest of his life trying to make up for the wrong he has done, even when a relentless police officer threatens to undo his good work. Talk about a remarkable story of redemption!

Les Misérables was both a theater and box office smash, not just because of the amazing musical score and script, but because audience members connected with Valjean's story. Perhaps you can as well. Like the kindly bishop, God has swept in and covered your debt. He has given you the opportunity to turn your life around, to make something good out of even the most shameful past. But the enemy of your soul is determined to stand in your way. He's relentless in his pursuit of you and wants to trip you up, psychologically and physically. He's that bitter police officer, ready to take you down.

Valjean never forgot the man he used to be, but he rose above the shame and anguish. You can do the same. Perhaps you've never been to prison. Maybe you've never stolen anything. Your shame may be rooted in something else altogether. But like Valjean, you can be set free from whatever lies behind you. All things are made new in Christ. You are a new creation with an amazing future.

Lord, I connect with Valjean on so many levels. You've given me countless opportunities. You've forgiven me over and over again. And yet I've betrayed You—with my words, my actions, my heart. Thank You for second chances. Thank You for restoration. I'm so grateful for Your love, Father. Amen.

No Condemnation

*There is therefore now no condemnation
for those who are in Christ Jesus.*
ROMANS 8:1

. . . .

The young man struggled to know the difference between conviction and shame. Free from his past addictions, Greg should have been living life with joy and zeal. He'd experienced grace from those he'd hurt and mercy from those he'd wronged.

But something held him back. Every time he thought about the sins of yesterday, he felt overwhelmed with guilt and shame. He couldn't seem to shake those feelings no matter how hard he tried. Sometimes the shame stopped him in his tracks. It kept him from moving forward, try as he may.

It took some time for him to realize this shame was an attack from the enemy, not conviction from the Lord. As he examined the scriptures, Greg discovered that God never intended anyone to feel condemned. Convicted, sure, for conviction leads to repentance. But condemned? Never.

What about you? Have you settled the issue in your heart? Do you know the difference between conviction and condemnation? Do you ever feel like you've swapped out one for the other? Things can get confusing sometimes.

Sure, you've done things in the past you wish you could

change. We all have. But your past does not define you, no matter how awful it might have been. When you live under a cloud of condemnation and shame, you never truly experience freedom. God longs for you to come out from under that cloud so you can share your testimony with others and live the amazing life He has planned for you.

Spend some time with the Lord today. Ask Him to show you the difference between His conviction (which played a lovely role in turning your story around) and the enemy's condemnation. It's time to cut off the condemnation once and for all.

Father, I get it now. I've been living under condemnation, thinking it was conviction. But You have come to set me free from my yesterdays so that I can be effective in my todays and tomorrows. No more shame, Lord. No more condemnation. I'm free to be all You have created me to be. Amen.

The Giver of Shame

*"The thief comes only to steal and kill and destroy; I have
come that they may have life, and have it to the full."*
JOHN 10:10 NIV

Where does shame come from? Is it thrust upon you by other
people? Is it something you choose to pick up and carry through
life, like a backpack or purse? Where does it come from and how
do you rid yourself of it?

You have a very real enemy, and according to 1 Peter 5:8, he
seeks to devour you. Think about that for a moment. That means
he won't stop until he's eaten you up and spit you out. If you had
a physical enemy—say, a neighbor or a coworker, one you could
see with your eyes—this notion would terrify you. But Satan isn't
visible, so you may forget he's at work behind the scenes.

Oh, but he is at work! And he's clever. He knows your weaknesses, knows just how to get his jabs in. He has studied your
movements and knows your vulnerabilities, so his moves are
calculated and swift.

One of the ways the enemy attempts to take you down is by
thrusting shame on you. He takes the pangs of conscience you
experience, twists and distorts those feelings, and showers you
with shame. It sticks to you like glue as he whispers words like,
"You're such a loser," or "You'll never get past who you used

to be," in your ear. He convinces you that you're no good, that God couldn't possibly love you, that you'll never overcome the shame of your past.

Here's the truth: God is not the author of shame. He longs for you to be set free and to see your accuser for who he is. Today, look the enemy in the face. See his tactics for what they are— carefully aimed arrows headed straight for your heart. Deal with any true conviction of the Holy Spirit, but don't give the enemy a foothold. He has no place in your thought life, in your present, or in your future.

I will be on my guard, Lord! I won't allow sneak attacks from the enemy. My eyes are wide open as I stand guard. When he tries to clothe me in shame, I will remind him that I am already dressed. . .in the full armor of God! Amen.

Who Gives Shame Power?

For if anyone is a hearer of the word and not a doer, he is like a man who looks intently at his natural face in a mirror. For he looks at himself and goes away and at once forgets what he was like. But the one who looks into the perfect law, the law of liberty, and perseveres, being no hearer who forgets but a doer who acts, he will be blessed in his doing.
JAMES 1:23–25

. . . .

Picture a political candidate moving up the ranks toward his office of choice. As the momentum builds, so does his motivation. Shoulders squared, speeches perfected, talking points developed, he begins to see himself as a force to be reckoned with. He's a man on a mission. Others begin to see him that way too, and nudge him along toward his goal, offering pats on the back and even monetary donations. In him they have found an ally, a cohort, a representative. This man *is* them, for all practical purposes.

Power is a remarkable thing. It energizes and motivates us, even changes our perspective. When we feel powerful, we're invincible, especially if we're surrounded by people who encourage us at every turn. Nothing can touch us when we feel this way.

That's why it's so important not to give shame power in your life. Once you go there, it's hard to turn back. Shame is like that political candidate—shoulders squared, eyes set on the prize of taking you down. If you're not careful, you'll end up supporting it with pats on the back. You'll make it your ally, your friend. It will begin to represent you.

God never intended for us to live in shame. He wants us to be set free from the past. Take a close look at today's scripture. When you look in the mirror, what do you see? Is the reflection staring back at you someone with the weight of shame on her shoulders, or do you see yourself as God sees you? It's time for a new way of seeing. Toss that old mirror and get a new one. And while you're at it, toss shame out the window too. Your entire perspective will shift when you get rid of it for good.

Shame is not your representative. Jesus Christ has taken care of that, once and for all.

Father, I have to admit, I've been giving shame power in my life. I've hoisted it to a place of honor. But, no more! I choose to toss my proverbial mirror and look only into Your face as I move forward, Lord. Amen.

The Spirit Bears Witness

The Spirit himself bears witness with our
spirit that we are children of God.
ROMANS 8:16

. . . .

You are a child of God. Pause to think about that for a moment. The King of the universe, the Author of all, is your Daddy. He's the One you run to with tears streaming down your face when you've fallen and scraped your knee. He's the first to rush to your defense when the other kids are picking on you. He's the One who tucks you in at night and gives you a kiss on the forehead before sending you off to school each day.

Your heavenly Father longs for you to accept the fullness of what it means to be His child. You're not an accidental family member. You're grafted in, bone of His bone, flesh of His flesh. He chose you, loves you, and wants the best for you, just as any parent would want for their beloved child.

With your adoption into the family comes the realization that you don't have to carry the pain or the shame of your yesterdays anymore. What a blessing to be rid of those things permanently! Can you imagine if your little one came to you, broken and repentant, ready for a second chance? Surely you would not turn your back on him. You would sweep him into your arms and kiss his little face, then give him every opportunity to begin again.

That's what loving parents do.

That's how it is with your heavenly Father too. He never meant for you to carry the shame of yesterday. No matter what you've done, no matter where you've been, no matter how low you've gone, He sees you as that precious child, ready to be scooped up into His arms and held tight. Once He's kissed away those tears, let Him refresh you and convince you that you have worth, you have a future. When you reach that point, His Spirit will truly bear witness with your spirit that you're His and He's yours.

I'm Your child, Father! You're my Daddy-God. Your arms are wide open, welcoming me, no matter what mistakes I've made. Your Spirit is like a witness in a trial, ready to speak on my behalf. How happy this security in You makes me feel. Amen.

Set Like a Flint

But the Lord God helps me; therefore I have not been disgraced; therefore I have set my face like a flint, and I know that I shall not be put to shame.
ISAIAH 50:7

. . . .

She knelt at the altar, tears streaming down her cheeks. For all of her attempts to maintain some degree of decorum, Hannah could not be quieted. The weight of her pain was too much to bear.

And so the tears flooded down her face and her heart twisted in a thousand pieces as she contemplated her lot in life. Would she ever give her husband a child? If not, would he begin to see her as useless, a woman of no value, simply because she had not given birth to an heir? Harder still, would Eli begin to prefer Peninnah, his other wife? This notion caused Hannah to agonize further. How could she ever show her face in public if Peninnah continued to ridicule her for her barrenness?

As she poured out her heart, shame wrapped itself around Hannah. "I'm not normal. I'm not like the other women I know. I can't do what they do. I can't have what they have. I'll never be what they are. This whole situation is totally unfair! Have I done something wrong to deserve a barren womb? Or is this just my lot in life? Why, Lord? Why?"

Perhaps you can relate to Hannah. Maybe you feel some

sense of shame because you're not like other women. You're not interested in the same things they're interested in. You look different, dress different, have a different way of doing things. Maybe those women—even within the walls of the church—have ridiculed you or ostracized you in some way. They've made you feel different, unaccepted, unloved.

You have intense longings and desires that reach to your core, but you wonder if God hears you. Like Hannah, you agonize apart from the crowd, knowing they would only make fun of you.

Today God wants you to know that there's no shame in uniqueness. He fulfilled Hannah's dream of giving birth to a son, and He will fulfill your dreams too, whether they line up with others' aspirations. In the meantime, be yourself. Learn to love who you are. You're created in the image of God, after all.

I might not be like other women, Lord, but I'm definitely like You! You created me, Your child, in Your image. I bear Your reflection and carry Your DNA. Thank You for creating me uniquely, Father. Amen.

The Joy Set before Him

Looking to Jesus, the founder and perfecter of our faith, who for the joy that was set before him endured the cross, despising the shame, and is seated at the right hand of the throne of God.

HEBREWS 12:2

. . . .

The young mother rocked her little one to sleep. Rising from the chair, she kissed his broad little forehead and lifted him into his crib. She glanced down at that precious face, overcome with love, but also overwhelmed with feelings of inadequacy.

Would she ever be enough? Could she really give this beautiful, special-needs child everything he needed to thrive? Or would she end every day like today, feeling like she didn't have what it took to see the journey from start to finish?

Other moms would have calmer, simpler lives in comparison. It hardly seemed fair at times, though she tried not to focus on that. Instead, she kept her hands on the wheel of this proverbial car she'd been given, and she drove like a maniac, one task after another.

In the quiet moments, she still questioned. . .everything. What would her journey look like? Could she accomplish all that would be required of her, or would she struggle to know how to cope with the doctor visits, the physical therapy, the special diet? Could she manage the communication methods, the medications, the meetings with teachers?

Millions of mamas face the joys and challenges of raising kiddos with special medical, psychological, and academic needs. If you're one of them, consider this a loving pat on the back and a rousing "You've got this, Mom!" Raising children is a tough gig, but throw in medical issues or genetic problems and things can get overwhelming in a hurry. That's why we need the body of Christ so desperately.

Here's the good news: God never intended for us to fit in. He longs for believers to stand out, to bring glory to Him. And that's exactly what all of these special-needs children do: they reflect Him—His love, His grace, His joy, and His affection. They shine like the stars they are and leave imprints far deeper than most.

So don't feel inadequate, Mom. You're doing a terrific job. You've got this!

Father, I thank You for every child in my life. Show me how I can help moms who are feeling overwhelmed with caregiving. I want to offer a hand so that they don't feel alone. May they never feel alone, Lord. Amen.

I Call on You

I call on you, my God, for you will answer me;
turn your ear to me and hear my prayer.
PSALM 17:6 NIV

. . . .

You never meant for this to happen. You did your best to be financially accountable. From the time you were young, you set aside money for a rainy day. While other kids spent their allowance on candy and toys, you remained diligent, faithful.

How could you have known an unforeseen medical crisis or the death of a marriage would leave you waist-deep in debt? You didn't cause your circumstances, after all. In fact, you never saw yourself in this position. Things like this happened to other people, not you.

Now the bill collectors are knocking at your door. The shame they inflict on you is cruel and unrelenting. Why won't they stop calling? You've told them what you're going through, but they just don't seem to care. Will they ever leave you alone, or will they continue to torment you, adding insult to injury? How can you make things right again?

You're not the first person to struggle with financial woes, nor will you be the last, but the ever-tightening coil of shame and fear can leave you feeling isolated, terrified, and hopeless. That's exactly where the enemy of your soul wants you to be, painted into a corner, frozen in place. God, on the other hand, wants to set you free from all of that. He doesn't just long for you to come out from under the cloud of shame; He wants to set you on a new path toward financial freedom.

Don't give up. You haven't seen the end of this journey. There is a way out. God has already made a plan, and His revelation will bring freedom. Tune yourself to His still, small voice so that you can be carefully guided out from the bondage. And while you're at it, go ahead and praise Him. If you can learn to lift Him up, even in the middle of the financial storm, your faith will be strengthened and He will be praised. Praise is the answer you've been seeking. It will set you free, one moment—one trial—at a time.

Father, I don't feel like praising You right now.
I feel so weighted down with these financial woes.
But today I make a willful choice to lift my hands, my heart,
and my spirit so that I can see the future as a hopeful place.
You've already set my feet on a road toward freedom.
Now, help me walk it out, I pray. Amen.

A Tree Planted by Streams of Water

That person is like a tree planted by streams of water,
which yields its fruit in season and whose leaf does
not wither—whatever they do prospers.
PSALM 1:3 NIV

As a father, he did his best to set a good example. His kids, for the most part, anyway, did well. All but one. Why this one headstrong teen was so set on following his own path was a mystery, but what could a father do but pray? It ripped his heart out to see his child suffer the inevitable consequences of his own actions, but allowing him to learn some lessons firsthand was for the best. No rescuing. No enabling from this dad, not if he could help it, anyway. No, he would step back and let the Holy Spirit do the work, hard as that might be.

Maybe you can relate to this brokenhearted father. You've done your best to raise your children to love God and respect themselves and others. But you have a straggler, a prodigal. He's not just content to run wild; he's on a mission to embarrass and humiliate your entire family. And he's doing a fine job of it.

There are times you want to hide away from your friends. . .the ones with the perfect kids. Sometimes these well-meaning folks inflict shame on you without meaning to. They brag about their kiddos' achievements or make comparisons. They carry on about their son's college of choice, his academic achievements, or his latest mission trip to Africa. And though there are no outward comparisons to your prodigal, sometimes you feel it. Keenly. You do your best not to let their words stick, but sometimes they do.

God understands what you're going through. Some of His kids are stragglers too. How it must break His heart to watch them wander from the narrow path. Like you, He's always right there, ready to lead them back home once their wandering is behind them.

Remember, life moves in seasons. Pray that your prodigal's season of wandering will be short and that he will learn the necessary lessons well. And remember, it's okay to celebrate your friend's child even when your own is causing you grief. Instead of comparing, learn to celebrate the victories of all of God's kids.

Father, sometimes I feel like I'm surrounded by prodigals. Family members, friends, neighbors, coworkers. So many have wandered from the safety of the fold and don't seem to care if they ever come back. I pray for all of the wanderers today, Lord. Turn their hearts toward home, I pray. Amen.

Guard That Day

But Stephen, full of the Holy Spirit, looked up to heaven and saw the glory of God, and Jesus standing at the right hand of God. "Look," he said, "I see heaven open and the Son of Man standing at the right hand of God."
ACTS 7:55–56 NIV

One of the most compelling New Testament stories takes place in the seventh chapter of the book of Acts. A powerful young man, Stephen, is about to be put to death for his public proclamation of the Gospel. He has done nothing wrong. In fact, he has done exactly what God called him to do. And now he's about to face eternal consequences.

Picture yourself in his shoes. If you knew the end was near, that you would soon be martyred for your faith, how would you respond? Check out Stephen's reaction:

When the members of the Sanhedrin heard this, they were furious and gnashed their teeth at him. But Stephen, full of the Holy Spirit, looked up to heaven and saw the glory of God, and Jesus standing at the right hand of God. "Look," he said, "I see heaven open and the Son of Man standing at the right hand of God." (Acts 7:54–56 NIV)

In that moment, Stephen caught a glimpse of heaven. Through the power of the Holy Spirit, he was able to catch a sneak peek even before that first stone was thrown. And what he saw changed his perspective entirely.

While they were stoning him, Stephen prayed, "Lord Jesus, receive my spirit." Then he fell on his knees and cried out, "Lord, do not hold this sin against them." When he had said this, he fell asleep. (Acts 7:59–60 NIV)

Why do you suppose God peeled back the corner of heaven and gave Stephen this little glimpse? Can you even imagine what he must have seen?

No doubt, the incident offered all the enticement Stephen needed to leave his situation behind and step into the beauty of heaven. In that moment, Stephen wasn't thinking about who he used to be, what evil deeds he might have done in his past. He wasn't fretting over how unfair his present circumstances were. He wasn't pointing fingers at his accusers. All thoughts of such things were behind him as he caught that first glimpse of eternity.

What a precious gift, the release of shame and blame. It frees us up to face this life and to prepare for the next.

Father, You've given me a tiny glimpse of eternity, and I like what I see. One day I'll be with You forever. Thank You for releasing me of my past so that I can share this beautiful "forever" with You, Lord. I'm looking forward to it with all my heart. Amen.

Take Your Thoughts Captive

We demolish arguments and every pretension that sets itself up against the knowledge of God, and we take captive every thought to make it obedient to Christ.

2 CORINTHIANS 10:5 NIV

. . . .

Shame is much like a tiny seed. If you plant it, give it attention, water it, nourish it, and pull up the weeds surrounding it, it will grow. Before long, a tiny sliver of shame has morphed into an overwhelming problem.

This is especially true when it comes to your thought life. The more you allow your thoughts to go there, the more you agonize over something or replay it in your mind, the bigger the issue gets. Before long, you're ashamed of everything—your thoughts, your actions, your inabilities. You're even ashamed of trying to look strong when you're really not. And sometimes you wonder if God is ashamed of you too.

First of all, God could never be ashamed of you. He adores you. And remember, He took your sin and shame upon Himself.

Second, He never intended for your thoughts to be tangled up. Take a closer look at this verse from 2 Corinthians. Pretension (falsehood) sets itself up against the knowledge of God. The enemy would love to twist your thinking and make you feel that everything is your fault or that you'll never measure up. That's his "pretense" to make you feel inadequate. But look what this scripture says. You can take authority over such lies by taking your thoughts captive, nipping shame in the bud.

So how do you take your thoughts captive? Don't rehearse them. Don't entertain them. Don't speak them aloud. The moment that thought flits through your mind, speak the Word of God instead. Speak life over your situation, not death. And don't allow the enemy to isolate you from others who will also speak life over you. Surround yourself with people who see you as an overcomer, not a failure. Before long, you'll see yourself that way too.

You can—and will—be set free. Begin to step out in that freedom even now.

Father, today I choose to take my thoughts captive. I won't allow myself to give in to despair or shame. I see that the enemy is trying to tangle my thoughts, but I won't let him. You've given me clarity of mind to live a powerful and productive life. I'm so grateful, Lord. Amen.

Whoever Believes in Him

As it is written, "Behold, I am laying in Zion a stone of stumbling, and a rock of offense; and whoever believes in him will not be put to shame."
ROMANS 9:33

. . . .

The problem begins in the mind. If you think you can't, you won't. If you think you'll be rejected, you will be. If you think you're not good enough, you'll live your life that way. If you think you're inherently flawed, you'll act out of that belief.

But how do you break free? If you spend days, weeks, years, decades caught up in negative thought processes, convinced you're a failure, you'll be paralyzed by fear before you even begin. It's not that you've actually stepped out, tried, and failed. You're afraid of taking that first step because your mind has convinced you you'll be an unmitigated disaster. So you remain frozen in place. Sure, you want to move forward, but fear of failure holds you captive, your feet frozen in place.

How do you get past what happens in the mind? How can you lay down that fear of failure? First, believe that God is on your side. He's the One nudging you out of the nest. Second, stop worrying about what other people think. Their opinions aren't yours to worry about. And so what if you stumble and fall? People do it every day. Others will see you as brave if you step out. Finally, don't try to hide your mistakes. People will appreciate your vulnerability if they see your imperfections.

The Bible says that you can be transformed by the renewing of your mind. That process begins with one simple act of submission. Tell the Lord you're ready for a thought transplant, a radical overhaul of your thought life. He's been waiting for you to come on board with that idea for a while now. Give Him your fear of failure. He can handle it. Then, as you do step out in faith, keep your eyes completely on Him. That way, if you do stumble (and you might), your gaze will be fixed solely on Him.

Lord, I'm tired of this negative thinking. I'm weary of being stuck. Fear is no friend of mine. It has held me back, and I'm tired of it. Thank You for renewing my mind and transforming my thought processes. I'll step out in faith, Father, with my eyes fixed on You. Amen.

For Freedom We Have Been Set Free!

For freedom Christ has set us free; stand firm therefore,
and do not submit again to a yoke of slavery.
GALATIANS 5:1

. . . .

John Newton's life took an abrupt turn when he entered into a relationship with Christ. This onetime slave ship captain renounced his former life and became an Anglican clergyman and abolitionist. Quite a radical transformation, one that didn't go over well with many of his colleagues. Not that John particularly cared about offending anyone with his newfound beliefs. His eye was fixed on the prize every step of the way.

Had he not taken a stand for freedom and equality, John Newton's legacy would have been a far different one. His heart was greatly troubled by the issue of slavery, which was still rampant in his day. Though it almost wrecked his health, his career, and his relationships, John took a stand against this abomination, insisting before his fellow political leaders that all were created in God's image and all deserved freedom. This was not a popular stand, to be sure, but he stood strong despite all opposition.

Perhaps you know John Newton best for the song he penned: "Amazing Grace." Hearing his backstory surely gives you a sense of why he felt so compelled to write a song about grace. John understood what many of us have not—it was for freedom that Christ set us free. He's not a slave ship captain, holding us hostage to fear and pain. Instead, He's the author and finisher of our faith who wants to set us free from bondage of any kind—emotional, financial, spiritual, and so on.

In particular, these lines from the song tell us how Newton felt about his own personal transformation: "I once was lost, but now am found. Was blind, but now I see."

The scales fell from Newton's eyes, and he could see. He had been blind to the plight of others and to God's opinion on slavery. But then, through the grace of the Almighty, he was set free.

God wants you to walk in freedom too. You don't have to stay married to the past. Don't submit to the yoke of slavery anymore. Step out into the sunlight and be free. It doesn't matter who you used to be, what you used to believe, or where you've come from. You can impact history in the same way Newton did, by taking a stand for what is right.

It is for freedom that You have set me free, Lord. I'm no longer bound. As the song "Amazing Grace" puts it, I once was lost, but now am found. I have clearer vision now, Father. It's Your amazing grace that has brought me this far, and I can't wait to see what You have ahead for me. Amen.

Out of Deep Waters

He reached down from on high and took hold of me;
he drew me out of deep waters.
PSALM 18:16 NIV

· ·

If you've ever faced powerful ocean waves firsthand, you know how terrifying they can be. Sometimes they catch you off guard and threaten to do you in. When you get out into deep waters, fighting against the pull of the waves, you wonder if you'll ever make it back to shore. You find yourself gasping for breath, pulled under, over, and all around. You feel completely powerless against the pull of the waves.

That same sensation is common when you're going through a crisis. And when you're in a season of compounded crises, when one tragedy strikes upon another, you might even feel like you're drowning. It's easy to give up when you're pulled out to sea like that. All hope seems lost.

Surely Job understood that feeling. This poor fellow found himself tossed and turned by waves that pummeled him half to death. When he reached his lowest point—facing the loss of loved ones, home, and health—Job easily could have given up. The proverbial ocean waves had taken their toll; he was a shell of a man, completely broken, filled with anguish.

But God.

God provided a lifeline back to shore. He offered hope. He removed any semblance of misplaced shame and gave Job reason to hope again, to dream again, to believe again. The sea calmed, and before long, all of the "lost" things in Job's life had been restored, and then some.

Job's story started well, took horrible twists and turns, but ended on a positive note. You can have that same happy ending if you don't give up before your miracle comes. No matter how strong the current, don't let anything stop you from believing God is on your side. He is, and He's your strongest defender, as He was for Job. Yes, you might be walking through a crisis right now, but better days are coming. Don't give in to the fear while you're waiting on the miracle.

Father, there are days when I feel like Job. Everything seems to be against me. I get so low that anguish and shame cover me like a dark cloud. I can't see my way out from under it. Then I'm reminded that Job found comfort and restoration at the end of his story. I'm waiting on my happy ending, Father, and I'll trust You in the meantime. Amen.

Never Ashamed!

I sought the LORD, and he answered me and delivered me from all my fears. Those who look to him are radiant, and their faces shall never be ashamed.
PSALM 34:4–5

. . . .

Not everyone felt that Marie Skłodowska deserved a shot at medical school. As she proceeded with her studies of physics, chemistry, and mathematics at the University of Paris, she faced harsh circumstances—financial woes, cold winters, lack of food, and scrutiny from those who felt she didn't belong. Beyond all of that was the ever-present opinion of some around her that women simply didn't belong in that world. They felt she should be home, finding a husband and bearing children. Only, Marie didn't feel called to that, at least not yet.

Marie earned a degree in physics in 1893 and went on to earn another in 1894. She would do everything in her power to prove her naysayers wrong. She wanted to prove to them that a woman could excel in her field, and she wouldn't stop until she'd convinced them.

When she met her husband-to-be, Pierre Curie, she found an ally, someone who appreciated her both romantically and academically. With his support, she went on to pursue a PhD. This collaboration worked on multiple levels, giving her the psychological boost she needed and a teammate with whom to work. Together, they were invincible. Marie became a physicist and a chemist (very rare for a woman in those days). She also pioneered the study of radiation. And all of this she did while battling naysayers.

What about you? Have you battled naysayers as well? Have they threatened to stop you before you could achieve success? Anytime negative voices try to shame you out of your God-given calling, you can confront them with confidence. And when the Lord brings an ally, as He did in Marie's case, you stand an even better chance of overcoming. There's nothing like having someone on your side. Even when you face scrutiny, stand firm.

If God has called you to a task, surely He will equip you for it. You have nothing to be ashamed of when God is the instigator. So hang in there. Who knows—you might have amazing discoveries in your future like Marie did.

Father, I won't give up, even if people around me offer words of negativity instead of encouragement. I don't need pats on the back to keep going. You've called me. You will equip me. All I need is You, Lord. Amen.

Reconciling All Things

And through him to reconcile to himself all things, whether on earth or in heaven, making peace by the blood of his cross.
Colossians 1:20

. . . .

The perfect life. The perfect surroundings. The perfect relationship with their Creator. Adam and Eve truly had it all. The word *paradise* seemed fitting for their new home. It offered humankind the first glimpse into God's handiwork and the first hope of eternity.

Oh, to have such close communion with the Creator. Can you imagine walking with God in the cool of the evening? Hearing His voice? Feeling His presence in every created thing around you? Can you imagine watching all of nature bow to the beauty and majesty of God? Hearing the sounds of the animals at peace around you? Listening to the rushing of waterfalls and the whistling of the wind through those remarkable trees?

Surely Adam and Eve experienced God's creative handiwork to its fullness. How they must have marveled at every blade of grass, every tiny doodlebug, every drop of morning dew.

Their very lives were miraculous on every level. Their bodies? Healthy and strong. Their potential? Endless.

Then, as with all flawed human beings, they took a tumble. Made a wrong decision. When temptation came, they sacrificed their perfect life in hopes of something better. Our minds reel as we think this through. How could they have expected more than what they already had, after all?

The repercussions of their actions have rippled across generations and affected us all. One decision—one horrible, rebellious, life-altering decision—changed everything for humankind. Can you even imagine the shame they must have felt as they stood naked before the Lord in the garden that fateful day? How broken their hearts. How somber their faces. Surely the fig leaves they sewed to cover themselves were as much symbolic as physical.

Maybe you've known the kind of shame that these two felt. You were caught. Uncovered. Undone. Your sin had major consequences, not just for yourself, but for others you loved as well. And there was no hiding, no getting away from what you'd done.

Before you throw in the towel, remember, God had a plan of redemption to resolve the problems sin caused. So don't give up. Give your shame to Him instead. He can take even the messiest problem and still point you toward eternity in paradise with Him.

Father, I've often traded in "good" for something I thought would be better. In the end, regrets abounded! I don't want to get caught up in the "good, better, best!" way of thinking.
I want to be satisfied with what You've given me.
May I keep my focus on You, Lord. Amen.

Taste and See

Oh, taste and see that the LORD is good!
Blessed is the man who takes refuge in him!
PSALM 34:8

· ·

Picture a dining room table decked out with the finest china and crystal. Your host has chosen his most expensive silverware. And those crystal goblets! You've never seen anything like them. The centerpieces take your breath away. Even the napkins look like something you'd find in a royal palace.

Large platters of food are carried in by servers, each one offering tempting aromas. Steak sizzling from the grill. Asparagus cooked to perfection. Baked potatoes loaded with all the condiments you could imagine. Fresh-baked bread slathered with butter, which is now dribbling down the edges. Apple pie hot from the oven, still bubbling. You can smell the cinnamon. It tickles your nose and makes you so hungry, you can barely wait to dive in. The anticipation is great, but the satisfaction of that first bite is even better. Ah, such delight! Has there ever been a finer meal?

As good as that meal might be, there is something far superior. When you spend time with the Lord, the aroma is His peace, His kindness, His favor. You take your first nibble of His goodness and you're won over.

In His presence, all of your cares are laid to rest. You place them at His feet, comforted by the fact that He is your burden bearer. Your shoulders, once weighed down with shame, are free to relax. Your heart, once heavy with worry and fear, is free to beat more evenly. Your feet, once bogged down in the mire of stress, are free to run.

Taste and see! Spend time in His presence today. Let Him prove how much He cares. Take refuge from the storm. Hide away with Him for a few hours and focus on His goodness. You'll never have a tastier meal.

I've tasted and seen that You are good, Father! A few minutes with You far exceeds even the finest meal served at the loveliest table. With all of the bad swirling around me, I feel so refreshed after giving my time and energies to a few precious hours with You, where my worries are put to rest and You cover me with Your goodness. How I love and appreciate Your presence, Lord. I'm so grateful. Amen.

We Shall Be Like Him

Beloved, we are God's children now, and what we will be has not yet appeared; but we know that when he appears we shall be like him, because we shall see him as he is.
1 JOHN 3:2

You've been struggling with this for as long as you can remember. It's buried so deep, you wouldn't even know how to voice it. But the truth is, you're secretly ashamed of your body. In fact, you've been secretly beating yourself up over it from the time you were a kid. You didn't see yourself as normal. You were too fat. You were too thin. Your hair was too frizzy. Your legs were too skinny, your knees knobby, your ears too big, your eyes too close together. You didn't do well in school. Teachers didn't like you. Kids made fun of you. You were the last one chosen for teams in gym class. You were a reject, a loser.

On and on the list went, until you nearly drove yourself crazy worrying about it all.

These troublesome problems followed you into adulthood, and now you're genuinely ashamed of the way you look in clothes, shoes, glasses, hairstyles, and so on. Nothing you try is good enough. Every outing is painful because it means you have to deal with the imperfections all over again. . .and in a public way. It's grueling. You wonder if anyone else notices your problem areas like you do, or if you're doing a decent job hiding them under clothing. And even if you could hide your physical flaws, what about the social awkwardness? Can you ever get past that and stop worrying about what others think about how you speak, how you look, how you respond?

Here's the truth: You are created in God's image. He designed you specifically. If you criticize the design, you're criticizing the Designer. He has made you like you are. . .on purpose. So stop fretting. You are like your heavenly Father, a true representation of Him. Sure, there will be tough outings. You won't always come away from every social event feeling like a winner. But you will grow over time, and God will show you how to overcome your insecurities if you'll step out in faith. In the meantime, relax and enjoy the ride!

I'm like You, Lord. I might not be perfect on the outside, but I'm created in Your image, and that truth brings peace to my soul. Help me to stop beating myself up, Father. I'm done with self-abuse. It's time for a fresh start. Help me, I pray. Amen.

That You May Know

I write these things to you who believe in the name of the Son of God, that you may know that you have eternal life.
1 JOHN 5:13

. . . .

You never meant for it to happen. But one foolish and impulsive act—driven by hormones—started you down a path of sexual sin. Once that door cracked open, you couldn't seem to turn back. Relationship after relationship, mistake after mistake, on and on you went. After a while, you hardly recognized yourself anymore. This was not at all how you envisioned your life going, and yet you couldn't seem to stop the ball of yarn from unraveling.

Before long, you found yourself in a place of shame you never expected. Others had harsh opinions of you too, but their perceptions paled in comparison to your own. You found it difficult to see yourself as anything other than ruined. In many ways, you felt painted into a corner with no way out. How could you erase the past and begin again?

Here's good news for all who've walked that difficult road: That broken young woman, no matter how scarred or how tainted, still has every opportunity to enjoy God's grace and mercy. She's the apple of His eye, the star in His crown. He longs to sweep her onto the proverbial dance floor and gaze into her eyes so that she can be assured, once and for all, of His love and favor. She's worthy of love, worthy of forgiveness, worthy of a chance to begin again.

If you're coming out of a similar situation, don't look back. You have eternal life now. Don't get wound up in your yesterdays, no matter how they tug at your conscience. Give yourself over to your todays and tomorrows instead. God wants you to know—really know—that you can have an eternal perspective. No more short-term thinking. No more hyper-focusing on mistakes. Your world is much bigger, much broader now, and His grace is broader still.

Rest easy in that grace today and believe. Truly believe.

Oh, how I long to be free from my yesterdays, Lord.
My actions were shameful. I don't even like to think of
them now. Instead, I'll maintain an eternity focus, Father.
What matters now isn't who I've been or what I've done,
but what You've done and where You're leading me.
I can't wait to see where that is, Lord. You have amazing
opportunities ahead, and I'm so grateful. Amen.

In the Wrestling Ring

For we do not wrestle against flesh and blood, but against the rulers, against the authorities, against the cosmic powers over this present darkness, against the spiritual forces of evil in the heavenly places.
Ephesians 6:12

Those who struggle with feelings of shame often convince themselves they are incapable of receiving love because they're not worthy. Think about that for a moment. Can you imagine a newborn baby coming into the world with feelings like this? Of course not. There's no way an infant would look into his mother's eyes and say, "Why don't you love me?" These are acquired feelings that develop over time as relationships grow complicated and complex. And they're aggravated by an enemy who loves to trip you up and make you feel unworthy.

You are worthy of love. You are worthy of relationship. You are worthy of a happy life. If none of these things were true, then why would Jesus have come to die for you? He loved you enough to risk everything. That's how much value you hold. That's how much He adores you. If anyone tries to convince you otherwise, step away from them in a hurry. There are enough trials in this life without adding the stronghold of shame. And remember what you're really wrestling with here: The enemy of your soul wants to trip you up. He doesn't want you to remember that the weapons of your warfare are intended to take him down. And his power is absolutely nothing in comparison to the power of Christ that lives in you.

What you could never do on your own, Jesus did for you when He sacrificed His life. He took your feelings of unworthiness and nailed them to the cross. He took those shameful feelings of "I don't fit in. They'll never accept me." Jesus dealt with all of it so that you wouldn't have to bear the heavy burden of shame. So why would you yoke yourself unnecessarily?

Anything you might be feeling today—inadequate, unworthy, unlovable—is a lie from the enemy. Jesus died to redeem you from all of those things. In Him, you are loved, you are worthy, you are enough. Don't let anyone tell you otherwise.

Father, I'm so glad for the reassurance that I am enough. You say I'm worthy. You say I'm lovable. You say I can move forward, away from feelings of inadequacy. Where would I be without You, Lord? I'm so grateful for Your assurance. Amen.

Abounding in Hope

May the God of hope fill you with all joy and peace in believing, so that by the power of the Holy Spirit you may abound in hope.
ROMANS 15:13

. . . .

He returned from war a broken man. PTSD became a constant struggle, though he didn't speak of it publicly. Guarded and afraid, this onetime soldier hid himself away, unwilling—or unable—to share his issues openly. Shame ruled the day whenever he took the time to assess his current struggles. Would people think less of him if they knew how tormented he was? Would they judge him if they knew he was bound up in fear?

Worst of all, would he ever get past this? Living in such bondage was taking its toll, after all. He found himself turning to alcohol or medication for comfort at times, something that tormented him further. But how could he ever adapt to his new normal? Should he have to?

Many come back from the battlefield feeling exactly this way. And you don't have to be a soldier to battle PTSD. Perhaps you're struggling with it now. You're on the far side of an abusive relationship, but you can't get past the fear. You've recovered from cancer, but you're terrified it will come back. You've been in a bad accident and you're on the road to recovery, but nightmares still abound. You've lost a loved one and you're still in a state of shock. It doesn't seem real. How will you ever adjust to your new normal?

PTSD is real, and it has held you locked in place. Like that soldier, you want to share your struggles with others, but they might judge you. So you decide to stick to yourself. This is, of course, exactly what the enemy wants you to do. He wants to isolate you and make you feel hopeless and alone.

It's time to acknowledge your struggle and to get the help you need (whether it's a support group, a counselor, a doctor, or a pastor). And don't forget to add prayer to the mix. Speak in faith over your situation. God longs for you to be set free from the agony of PTSD. Open your heart to new possibilities and watch Him move.

Lord, I don't want to be locked in place, frozen by fear. I'm tired of feeling this way. Today I ask You to intervene, to show me a path out of this PTSD I've been struggling with. Lead me to those who can help so that I might be healed. Amen.

A Shield around Me

But you, LORD, are a shield around me, my glory,
the One who lifts my head high.
PSALM 3:3 NIV

King George VI (Albert Frederick Arthur George) faced more challenges than the usual British king. He is remembered not just for being the father of the current queen of England, but for a particular challenge he faced while in office.

"Bertie" (as he was known among his family and friends) had not expected to inherit the throne. The unique opportunity presented itself when his elder brother, Edward, fell in love with a married woman. Talk about a scandal! Because Edward wasn't deemed suitable for the crown, Bertie had no choice but to take his place. This would-be king was terrified, to say the least. He never felt worthy of the crown and lived in constant fear that he would disappoint his people. To make things more difficult, the people had a hard time picturing him as their ruler as well.

Chief among Bertie's struggles was a stammer he couldn't seem to conquer. He was in no way responsible for this condition, but it brought him a tremendous amount of shame and embarrassment, particularly when he had to address the nation via radio. Talk about difficult! To convey his message to his people was critical, but the fear before each recorded event must have been overwhelming.

Working with a speech therapist helped, but Bertie never fully overcame his speech impediment. Still, he never gave up. He finally managed to get past the embarrassment of his condition and rule his people with strength and courage. He went on to give great speeches and to lead his people well. Overcoming his shame and pain was a triumph.

Perhaps you can relate on some level. Like Bertie, you're struggling with something you can't hide from others. Weight gain. Acne. An oddly shaped nose. A limp. A stammer. You're worried about what people will say, what they will think. It's time to stop fretting over the responses of others and just be yourself. Take a lesson from the king of England. Some personal struggles are meant to be shared openly so that others can learn by example.

I can't hide away forever, Lord. Like Bertie, I have my flaws, and they're visible to a watching world. Show me how to live boldly, without shame, so that I can impact lives by simply being myself. I want to be a living reflection of You, Father. Amen.

My Hiding Place

You are my hiding place and my shield;
I hope in your word.
PSALM 119:114

. . . .

Remember, as a small child, how you would hide whenever you felt ashamed? Maybe you broke your sibling's toy and knew Mom would be upset, so you hid under your bed. Or maybe you disobeyed your dad and knew there would be consequences, so you hid in the closet. Even toddlers who have potty-training accidents hide themselves behind furniture so that Mom doesn't find out what they've done. Hiding is in the nature of the fallen child because he fears his parents' response.

When it comes to God, though, you don't have to be afraid. Even if you're feeling like a disobedient child today, He's still chasing you down with the words "Don't run! Don't hide!" on His lips. Besides, He knows where you are at all times, so running is futile. You might as well give in to His love. If there's any hiding to be done, do it under the shadow of His wings, where He longs to protect you from harm.

God wants you to know that He adores you and forgives you, even when you're convinced you've gone too far. No sin is too big, no shame too great, no issue too fragile that you can't take it to God. He is longing to meet with you, even now.

The next time you feel like running, stop. Turn around. Look Him in the eye. No head-hanging. No stammering. Just trust that He still loves you regardless of what you've done. And also remember that you're in this relationship with your heavenly Father for the long haul. You're going to be spending eternity with Him, so it's better to keep things out in the open than to hide away.

Be brave. Share truth. He'll love you anyway.

Father, I'm so glad I don't have to hide from You when I mess up. I'd be hiding all the time. You're always right beside me, wooing me, asking me to open up and share my struggles with You, Lord. Here I am, approaching Your throne to repent of my wrongdoings and to ask for Your grace and mercy once again. Thank You for offering me Your forgiveness, Father. Amen.

Everyone Who Believes

For the Scripture says,
"Everyone who believes in him will
not be put to shame."
ROMANS 10:11

. . . .

The story of Rahab is one that still mesmerizes readers all these years later. The notion that God could—and would—use a prostitute to rescue His people is a bit of a shocker. If you had written the story, perhaps you would have chosen differently. You might've picked a stellar member of the community, someone well loved and respected. But isn't it just like the Lord to use someone like Rahab instead of the homeowners association president or PTO mom? He always uses the foolish things to confound the wise. And doesn't it bring a smile to your face to realize that He can handle things in His own special way, without asking our opinion?

Rahab, who worked as a prostitute, lived in the city of Jericho. Breaking loyalty with her own people, she assisted the Israelites in capturing Jericho. In doing so, she had to turn her back on her neighbors and friends and put her trust in the people of God. The risk was great, but she chose to help the Israelites at the risk of her own safety. For this reason, she is listed in the lineage of Jesus. (Wow, think about that!)

Whether we want to admit it or not, God can (and will) use

whomever He pleases. He was pleased to use Rahab, to plant her firmly in the history books as a heroine, not a villain. And He can use you too, no matter where you've been or what shame you've faced.

Aren't you glad the Lord doesn't discriminate? He adores all of us, with all of our warts, freckles, and poor choices. Looking back over your life might cause you to cringe, but sometimes it's important to realize how far you've come.

Rahab went on to be known as a woman who was righteous for her works. The same will be said of you once you finally let go of the past and allow God to place you in His great history book as a person of great faith.

Lord, You and I both know that my past isn't lily white. I've done some things I'm not proud of. But I'm encouraged by this story of Rahab. If You could use her to rescue the Israelites, You can use me to reach out to people who need to know You. May my past be a catalyst, not a deterrent, Father. I'm so grateful You've found me useful. Amen.

He Bore Our Shame

*He was despised and rejected by men, a man of sorrows
and acquainted with grief; and as one from whom men hide
their faces he was despised, and we esteemed him not.*
ISAIAH 53:3

· ·

Picture a man in a dark black cloak. He wears it everywhere. It drives his wife and kids crazy. He wears it to the movies, out to dinner, to the park, on vacation, to the beach. He keeps it on when he showers, when he sleeps at night, and when he shows up at the breakfast table.

This man is identified by all he comes in contact with by this cloak. The neighbors, his coworkers, his extended family members, others in the community. . .everyone recognizes this fellow with just a glance. They tend to shy away from him because he seems unapproachable. The cloak itself is the great separator. It's gloomy and frightening to look at, and makes him appear dirty. And the smell! Ugh. Does he even realize how bad the aroma is? He doesn't seem to care about any of that, though, which makes no sense at all. Why doesn't he just toss it into the trash can where it belongs?

Sound a little odd? That's exactly what it's like when you choose to put on the cloak of shame. It's as if you are choosing to be recognized for something other than who you really are.

You're deliberately adopting a stinky, grimy existence.

Stop to think about all that God has delivered you from. He has set you free from the pain, the sin, the sorrow of yesterday. He has delivered you out of the darkness into His glorious light. Why, then, would you choose to re-cloak yourself, to wear a reminder of who you used to be? It's not your identity anymore.

Sure, you did things you're not proud of. Yes, you wish you could unravel some of the mess. But God hasn't called you to take steps backward. He wants you to move forward, completely free. So toss that cloak! Put it in the trash where it belongs and walk in complete freedom in Christ.

Father, thank You for setting me free. I won't wear the cloak of shame anymore. I won't let others dress me in it, and I'll be on the lookout for the enemy of my soul because I know he's on the prowl. Thank You for setting me free. I'm happy to walk in Your freedom, Lord. Amen.

Don't Throw It Away

*Therefore do not throw away your confidence,
which has a great reward. For you have need of
endurance, so that when you have done the
will of God you may receive what is promised.*
HEBREWS 10:35–36

. . . .

Every athlete sets out to win the game. A competitive spirit runs strong from the moment he first steps onto that track, field, or court. To him, it's not just about beating the other guy. It's about bettering himself—going higher, farther, faster, stronger.

As he trains, this remarkable athlete is not just thinking of that next game; he has his eye on the ultimate prize—winning championships, one after the other. His confidence is bolstered by every new achievement. Before long, he sees the unattainable as possible, even probable. This change in thinking is critical if he's going to go the distance.

That's what faith will do. It gives you supernatural vision to see the impossible as possible. It will give you courage to believe for the impossible.

Consider the sport of figure skating. In 1882, a man by the name of Axel Paulsen invented a rotation jump with one and a half turns. Spectators were mesmerized by his amazing capabilities. How could he possibly leap into the air, spin around one and a half times, and land on one foot without falling? It seemed miraculous to them.

Jump ahead a hundred years or so to the modern Olympics. It's nothing for a competitor to land a triple axel, something that would have been unheard of in Paulsen's day. But the sport has progressed. Records have been broken. People have pushed themselves to new limits. Perspectives change. Growth takes place.

That's how it is with your faith. The harder you work at something, the more "possible" it becomes. You start out small, your faith unsteady. As God answers your prayers, that faith begins to grow. Before long, you're praying and believing for miracles.

Where do you stand today? Are you working on your single axel or your triple? Wherever you are, don't let go of your confidence. Allow God to bolster it so that you see the impossible as totally possible.

Father, I want my faith to increase over time, not decrease.
May I push the limits until I fully anticipate the unattainable
with You, Lord. I want to be like that athlete, getting stronger
and braver with time. May my faith increase as I inch
my way toward the ultimate prize. . .heaven! Amen.

Abound in Hope

May the God of hope fill you with all joy and peace in believing, so that by the power of the Holy Spirit you may abound in hope.
ROMANS 15:13

. . . .

She could hardly stand to look in the mirror these days. Sixty-plus years of life had changed her physique, and not in a good way. Body parts that used to be firm now sagged like worn pillows. Wrinkles in her thighs, belly, and backside made her groan. And she couldn't bear the thought of putting on a bathing suit during the summer months. What would people say if they saw her out in public looking like that? Surely the grandkids would be mortified to see Grandma at the pool, even in a modest bathing suit and towel.

Still, what could she do? Plastic surgery was out of the question, and exercise hadn't fixed the problem. Should she just plow forward with this sagging body and hope things didn't get worse? Should she hide herself away and anguish in private? Or should she reach for a gallon of ice cream to wash away her troubles?

The truth is we all age. If you study the scriptures closely, you'll see that silver hair and wrinkles are a badge of honor, not something to be ashamed of. And how would you prevent them, anyway? Hollywood stars and starlets have taught us firsthand that plastic surgery often leaves you looking like someone other than yourself. So which is worse—wrinkles or an identity change that will leave folks scratching their heads and saying, "Now, why did she think she needed to do that?"

What's the problem with sagging, anyway? The Bible says, "Though our outer self is wasting away, our inner self is being renewed day by day" (2 Corinthians 4:16). Don't lose heart! Your inner self is strong, firm, in tip-top shape! In fact, you're probably stronger in your faith today than you were in your twenties. And your perspective on life has grown over the years too, giving you a clearer view of what's really important.

That aging body of yours is a testimony, not something to be ashamed of. So celebrate those wrinkles. Flaunt that silver hair. You're a walking, talking example to those who are younger, after all. They're looking to you to lead the way.

I'll do my best not to be ashamed of this aging body, Lord.
Sure, things are shifting. And yes, I'm not as pleased with the
reflection in the mirror as I once was. But I do see that
You've done a great work on the inner me,
and for that I'm very grateful. Amen.

Change of Heart

For whenever our heart condemns us, God is greater than our heart, and he knows everything. Beloved, if our heart does not condemn us, we have confidence before God.
1 John 3:20–21

. . . .

Many believers throughout time have undergone radical transformations that caught the attention of people worldwide. One such person was Nicky Cruz, former gang member turned evangelist. The onetime leader of the infamous New York City gang, the Mau Maus, Cruz was known among his peers (and his enemies) as a warlord. He'd inched his way to the top of the group, a fierce leader.

Enter David Wilkerson, a passionate young evangelist, on fire for Jesus and ready to reach the Mau Maus with the Gospel message. Wilkerson arranged an evangelistic meeting at a local boxing arena, where he hoped to convert the gang members. How he managed to talk them into coming was nothing short of a miracle.

As he sat in the arena that night, Nicky Cruz's heart was touched by the Holy Spirit. No doubt he began to feel remorse for the many poor choices he had made, both in the Mau Maus and beyond. Before the night was over, Cruz responded to an altar call, and the rest is history. When Wilkerson prayed with Nicky, the two bonded and remained friends. Cruz went on to study the

Bible, even attending Bible college.

No doubt there were people who doubted Nicky's conversion or attempted to shame him for his former life. He had done some pretty awful things, after all. If he ever felt ashamed, Nicky never let that hold him back. He made it his mission to convert gang members to Christ and even led the Mau Maus' leader to the Lord.

Can you imagine how this story might have been interrupted if Nicky had allowed shame over his former life to hold him back? It might have stopped him in his tracks. That's exactly what the enemy wants—to stop believers from moving forward by causing them to doubt their worthiness. Don't let him stop you. Keep on going. The place you're headed is a far better place than where you've come from.

Father, You care about everyone, no matter where they come from or what they've done. I'm so glad You reach down and rescue even the toughest cases. Thank You for loving us all equally, Lord. Amen.

Steadfast

Blessed is the man who remains steadfast under trial, for when he has stood the test he will receive the crown of life, which God has promised to those who love him.

JAMES 1:12

. . . .

One doctor visit after another. No relief in sight. The woman—pale, anemic, embarrassed, ashamed—did everything in her power to get her bleeding issue under control, but nothing seemed to work. Would she just have to live like this for the rest of her life? If so, how would she bear it? This horrible condition separated her from those she loved, and it kept her from living a productive life. The situation was wholly unfair.

In a moment of sheer desperation, the woman crawled through a crowd of people to get to a man known for healing. Jesus. She knew little about Him, only that He might have some miraculous powers to heal her fragile body. And right now, that was the only thing on her mind, even if it meant risking public humiliation. She could deal with that, if what they said about this man was true.

It took some doing, but she pushed her way along until she saw His feet. His sandals. His legs. The hem of His garment. With the mob pressing in around her, it was now or never. She reached out and touched His hem, and then everything came to a halt.

"Who touched me?" Jesus' voice rang out. "I felt healing

power go out from me" (see Luke 8:45–46 NLT).

For a moment, she felt fear. Then, just as quickly, another feeling took over. Extreme joy! Just one touch and she had been healed instantly!

Then the woman, knowing what had happened to her, came and fell at His feet and, trembling with fear, told Him the whole truth. He said to her, "Daughter, your faith has healed you. Go in peace and be freed from your suffering" (see Luke 8:48). In one instant, all of her fears were gone. She had been completely set free—from her pain, her suffering, her embarrassment, and her shame.

Maybe you've been in a place of desperation like this woman. Perhaps fear of what others might think has held you back. Today is your day! Rush to Jesus. Touch the hem of His garment. Then watch as He stops everything to make sure you know how very loved you are.

Father, I've been in low places before. I've wondered if anyone noticed my pain or anguish. There were days when I might have been willing to crawl through a crowd on my hands and knees to find the answers I needed. I'm so glad You're here for me, Lord! I praise You. Amen.

Vulnerable

But he said to me, "My grace is sufficient for you, for my power is made perfect in weakness." Therefore I will boast all the more gladly of my weaknesses, so that the power of Christ may rest upon me. For the sake of Christ, then, I am content with weaknesses, insults, hardships, persecutions, and calamities. For when I am weak, then I am strong.
2 CORINTHIANS 12:9–10

. . . .

She knows how to hit where it hurts. Many times over she has brought accusations to the same areas of your life. You're not a good enough parent. You're too fat. You're not smart enough. You're a terrible wife. You'll never be able to hold down a job.

On and on she goes, cutting you down and making you feel useless. You know her words aren't true, but they still jab like knives in your flesh, and you don't know how to get past them. You wish you could push her words aside, ignore them, even nudge her out of your life. . .but you can't seem to. She's an ever-present critic, ready to jab you again and again.

We all have critics in our lives. Many of them have crossed the line on more than one occasion. Their words tear at the fiber of our being and cause us to question everything, including our worthiness. In short, they make us feel like failures.

It's time to break the chain between the critics and your

heart. Sure, there are areas of your life where you're particularly vulnerable. Maybe you're not the best housekeeper. Maybe you really do struggle with your weight. But that doesn't give anyone the right to inflict shame or blame. You alone are responsible for your life, your actions. With God's help, you'll make progress. But allowing someone to fling arrows at your heart will only slow you down, and you don't need that.

You have things to do, after all. So step back. Examine the relationship. If you're in a verbally or mentally abusive situation, you might have to sever the relationship altogether. Ask God to give you wisdom so that you can be set free from the negativity and shame.

Father, I'm so tired of being criticized. It feels like I'm always on the receiving end of the critique. Nothing I do is good enough. But You say I'm enough. You say I'm loved. Today I choose to believe Your words over the words of my critics. Your words bring life, and I need that today. Amen.

From the East to the West

As far as the east is from the west,
so far does he remove our transgressions from us.
PSALM 103:12

. . . .

Remember as a kid how fascinated you were with globes? It was so fun to spin that tilted blue orb and let your finger fall on a spot far away from where you lived. You would dream of visiting that exotic place someday, of traveling to unknown realms to see how other people lived. It all seemed so exciting back then. (And didn't the world seem smaller when you looked at it on the globe?)

Looking at that globe also put things in perspective. For the first time, you could see that your corner of the world was just a teensy-tiny spot, microscopic when you considered it as part of the whole. In fact, you had to search carefully to find it amid all of the other continents and oceans.

Even as an adult, you still see the world as a fascinating place. You've come to understand that it's much larger than it appeared when you were a child. There are thousands of miles between the North Pole and the South, between Texas and India, between England and Australia. To travel to these places would take hours, if not days, depending on your mode of transportation. You get overwhelmed just thinking about it.

When you ponder the vastness of planet Earth, when you

consider the great distance between point A and point B, do you marvel at God's ability to care for all of His kids, no matter where they live? And do you see how great a gift forgiveness is? When God says He casts your sin as far as the east is from the west, He's tossing it from California to the southernmost tip of Africa. He's sending it reeling from New Zealand to Spain. Wow! That's quite a distance.

Picture your sin taking a road trip to a place you'll never visit. God wants you to forget it—forget the shame, the agony, the remorse—all of it. Rest in the truth that His forgiveness is enough.

Father, I love this image that You're taking my sin on a road trip. You're doing away with it once and for all. You've sent it to the uttermost depths, never to be seen again. Thank You for this amazing work of forgiveness, Lord. Amen.

Shame for the Wicked

O Lord, let me not be put to shame, for I call upon you;
let the wicked be put to shame; let them go silently to Sheol.
Psalm 31:17

Anger and jealousy rose like a dark cloud over the group of brothers. They stared at the youngest—Joseph—in disdain as he stood before them in his colorful coat, a gift from their father. How long would the little braggart go on singing his own praises? Why did he have to share all of his dreams with them? Were they really to believe they would one day bow before him? What a pain in the neck this kid was turning out to be. Somebody needed to put him in his place, and soon.

Sure, Joseph was the pride and joy of their father, Jacob. No doubt about that. Well, the time had come to do something about it. They came up with a plan to kill him. If not for the oldest brother, Reuben, speaking up, Joseph would have died then and there.

Instead, the brothers threw Joseph into a pit. Reuben had a secret plan to rescue him later. Only, later never came. While Reuben was away, the other brothers sold Joseph into slavery to a company of Ishmaelite merchants. Later, they dipped Joseph's coat in blood and told their father that he had been torn apart by wild beasts. Jacob was inconsolable. This is where their bitterness and jealousy led them, down a path of complete destruction.

Can you imagine how those brothers felt as they attempted to move on with their lives? Surely they wondered about Joseph, tried to figure out whatever became of him. Perhaps they were riddled with shame and remorse for what they had done to him. Only when they met up years later did they finally realize God had honored Joseph's dreams and given him a position of authority in Egypt.

Maybe you can understand the plight of Joseph's siblings. Maybe you've struggled with jealousy too. Perhaps you've even hurt someone you love because you were jealous. There's still time to turn your story around. You can make things right now, before any more damage is done.

Father, I'm sorry for the many times I've been jealous of others. I'm especially sorry for the times I allowed my envy to cause problems for those I love. Please help me to make things right. The sooner the better, Lord. Amen.

Double Portion

*Instead of your shame there shall be a double portion;
instead of dishonor they shall rejoice in their lot;
therefore in their land they shall possess a double
portion; they shall have everlasting joy.*
Isaiah 61:7

She wore her scars in private, covering them with a cloak of shame as if she herself had somehow caused them. Years of abuse at the hands of another ate at her. She hadn't meant for the abuse to become her identity, but that's what had happened. She seemed to eat, sleep, and drink her pain.

Feeling completely stuck, she tucked herself away in cobweb-filled corners and prayed no one would ask about the tears in her eyes or her slouched shoulders. To open up, to share her story, would be too much. It would peel back the scab and cause more pain than she could bear. What good would that do? She would rather hide away and keep the pain to herself. At least there, no one could hurt her anymore. She was safe. Alone, but safe.

Perhaps you know this woman. Maybe you've been her. Coming out of an abusive situation is a grueling process. . .for a thousand reasons. So many women (and men) live in fear after the fact, afraid the abuse will somehow start up again. Many are cloaked in shame, though they were in no way to blame. For many, blame has been thrust upon them, like hand-me-down clothes on a broken-spirited child. As cruel and heartless as the abuse was, the abuser's accusations that followed only made things worse.

This kind of shame is a direct work of the enemy as he speaks through abusers: "This was all your fault!" "You don't deserve anything better than this!" "No one else will want anything to do with you!" Those words are filled with malice, not love.

No matter where you are in your journey today, know that God adores you. He longs to see you healed and whole—physically, emotionally, and psychologically. Cry out to Him and to those safe people He's placing in your life. Get the help you need, and then take the time to heal.

Father, how does a person recover from abuse? The pain is so intense and the fear is palpable. Help me to help those I love who are going through this, Lord. I want to intervene and play a role in restoring the lives of those experiencing the aftermath of abuse. Guide me, I pray. Amen.

Pleasing in Your Sight

May these words of my mouth and this meditation of my heart be pleasing in your sight, Lord, my Rock and my Redeemer.
PSALM 19:14 NIV

. . . .

Lydia made a few mistakes along the way. Her temper flared at times. She was distracted. Overextended. Tired. Her mothering skills paled in comparison to those of some other women she knew. Not that she was really trying to keep up with anyone. Lydia had enough trouble keeping up with her own stuff. Between the cranky boss, the overworked husband, the home repairs, and her own personal health issues, she could barely stay afloat.

Sure, the kids seemed fine. They didn't really notice her lack as much as she did, but sometimes—in the wee hours of the night—she felt it keenly, especially when her arthritis went into a flare. Would she ever have the wherewithal to give her children all they needed from her? Or would she always feel like she came up short when she compared her mothering skills to those of her friends and family members?

Maybe you can relate to Lydia's struggles. If you're attempting to raise kids while juggling a job, household chores, kids' activities, and so on, then you know it's nearly impossible to keep up at times. Maybe you're like Lydia in that you've stopped trying to keep up due to exhaustion or illness. Other mothers have their act together, but you? You're never going to succeed. The enemy has convinced you of that. In his usual, tricky way, he presses shame onto your shoulders, as if nothing you do will ever be good enough, which causes you to want to give up.

It's time to toss that shame to the curb. Sure, you need to do your best, but don't stress when you come up short. No mother on the planet is perfect (despite her social media status updates). Every mom feels inadequate. So square those shoulders. Lift that chin. Look your situation straight in the eye and move forward with the confidence that God has got your back.

Father, I'm no supermom. And I'm tired of trying to look like one. Help me do my best, and take up the slack where my abilities leave off, I pray. When I'm not feeling well, please give me strength. I'm trusting in You to help me raise these kids in a way that brings honor to Your name. Amen.

A Way of Escape

No temptation has overtaken you that is not common to man.
God is faithful, and he will not let you be tempted beyond your
ability, but with the temptation he will also provide the
way of escape, that you may be able to endure it.

1 Corinthians 10:13

Nothing is worse than living in the shadows, hiding your struggles from others. You do your best to act normal in front of friends and family members, but then those old temptations strike and you feel helpless, so you slink back into the depths once again, where you're free to do as you please without watchful eyes or critique. In that private place, you don't feel judged.

Not that you're proud of yourself for your poor choices. You're beating yourself up enough already. You don't need others to join in the party. Besides, they don't get it. They think you're doing this on purpose. How can you get them to understand: you've tried your best to escape, but you feel trapped.

So when you're out in public, around others, you plaster on a smile. You act like everything's okay. When they ask, you say, "I'm doing great, thanks!" But on the inside, you're battling those same old temptations. You're falling apart at the seams. And you're too afraid to let people in so that someone can help you.

There is hope! No matter how many times you've fallen, you

can get back up again. There's no shame in admitting you've taken a tumble. It's more awkward to pretend everything's okay than to come clean.

So come clean. Tell someone what you're dealing with. Don't let another day go by without confiding in someone. You need the accountability and prayer support of a friend right now—not someone to offer critique, but someone who will truly walk alongside you in your struggle toward your ultimate healing. Instead of fretting over how your accountability partner will feel once she knows what you're dealing with, focus on the fact that you'll have an accountability partner.

God has provided a way of escape for you. No one is more excited to see you break from your struggle with this temptation than He is. This temptation will not overtake you. Run toward freedom.

Father, I'm so grateful for a way of escape. Please point me in the direction of a mentor or friend who will hold me accountable. I need that hand to hold right now. Thank You for giving me a way out, Lord. Amen.

Dwelling in Safety

In peace I will lie down and sleep,
for you alone, LORD, make me dwell in safety.
PSALM 4:8 NIV

· ·

As a teen, Maggie tried hard to keep solid boundaries. Despite her best attempts, however, she kept getting coerced into doing things she didn't want to do. Run for student council? Sure. Work backstage on the school play? Okay. Serve on the prom committee? Why not?

Sometimes she felt like she had the word *sucker* on her forehead. And to top things off, she seemed to be a magnet for losers. Guys she would never consider dating were drawn to her for some reason. They said the right things. . .at first. But over time, their true colors came out.

This problem continued into her adulthood. She entered into one relationship after another with troubled men—addicts, men with temper issues, guys who couldn't hold down a job. She found herself feeling trapped more times than she could count. And she still kept getting talked into things—like letting that one guy move in with her when he lost his job.

Things weren't much better at work. In spite of her attempts to say no to her boss's unreasonable demands, she could not convince him to back off. He continued to expect more and more of her. Late hours. A crazy work schedule. On call at all times, even holidays. It was just too much.

By the time she reached her early thirties, Maggie was absolutely exhausted and ashamed of herself for her inability to say no to people. Why did she have so much trouble with such a simple little word? Others said no, and their lives were better off because of it. Would she ever say it. . .and mean it? Only when she took the time to realize the "why" behind her choices was she able to be set free.

Perhaps you've struggled like Maggie. You constantly find yourself trapped in situations you wish you could get out of. Instead of beating yourself up, get to the root of why you can't seem to say no. Deal with the real issue once and for all. Then take the "No!" pledge. Learn to say no. . .and mean it. If you're a people pleaser, repent and ask God to show you how to please Him first. When you do that, the need to say yes to everything will slowly fade away.

Father, I need better boundaries. I confess, I've had a hard time saying no to people. Please help me let go of the need to please the people around me, I pray. The only One I want to work to please is You. Amen.

Blessed Assurance

*Now faith is confidence in what we hope for and
assurance about what we do not see.*
HEBREWS 11:1 NIV

. . . .

The great hymn writer Fanny Crosby authored dozens of the great hymns we know and love, including "Blessed Assurance." Her life was anything but ordinary. She faced multiple struggles but didn't let them get her down or keep her from fulfilling the call of God on her life.

Fanny was stricken blind at six weeks of age when mustard poultices were applied to treat discharges from her eyes. They destroyed her optic nerves and stole her sight. Miraculously, she never seemed depressed by her inability to see. In fact, she considered her blindness a gift and referred to it often as such. (What a remarkable perspective!)

Fanny lived in physical darkness all of her life but had clear vision when it came to her faith. Her soul was on fire for Jesus. In Him she found the "vision" that she longed for. Others might have used that physical challenge to hide away, to stay secluded. But not Fanny. An avid musician, she played multiple instruments, including the piano, organ, harp, and guitar. She also had a lyrical soprano voice, which served her well as her career progressed.

Can't you picture her now, singing, *"Blessed assurance, Jesus* is mine! Oh, what a foretaste of glory divine! Heir of salvation, purchase of God. Born of His Spirit, washed in His blood." What a glorious moment that must have been, hearing Fanny sing those words for the very first time. Some songs cut straight to the heart.

And talk about talented! Fanny started writing early on and went on to become the most prolific American hymn writer of the nineteenth century. She never let her inability to see stop her from becoming all she was created to be.

What about you? Have you let anything stand in your way of becoming all God is asking you to be? Perhaps this is the day to separate the wheat from the chaff, to see what stays and what goes, so that you're free to follow after God wholeheartedly with the gifts He has given you.

Father, I want to be all You've called me to be. I won't let my limitations cause shame or embarrassment. I'll follow Fanny's lead and make myself useful, even though I have imperfections. Thanks for using me, Lord. Amen.

Rejoicing in Your Salvation

But I trust in your unfailing love; my heart rejoices
in your salvation. I will sing the LORD's praise,
for he has been good to me.
PSALM 13:5–6 NIV

. . . .

There's reason to celebrate!

Picture a prisoner, one who's been living in the confines of a dank, dark prison cell for years. He's finally being set free. Walking outside into the sunlight that first time, he's blinded by the light. Once his eyes adjust, he's overcome with emotions—joy, peace, excitement, and a thousand other feelings, besides. At first, he hardly knows which way to go—to the right? The left? Straight ahead? Every decision has been made for him over the past several years, after all. From this point on, he gets to call the shots. He can only hope he'll call the right ones.

Unsure of himself, he takes a tentative step forward. It feels great. Before long, he's bounding down the sidewalk, a free man, ready to face his new life and to explore worlds yet unknown.

If you've been set free from sin and shame, you know exactly what this man is going through. Coming out from under the cloud of shame can be as complicated as leaving a prison cell. You've never operated without it before. But God has set you free—completely free. No more bondage for you. No more pain. No more hiding away from the crowd, tucked under the umbrella of guilt and fear. . .and that's reason to celebrate!

So how will you step out in faith now that shame is no longer there to define you? Will you tell others? Will you share your story publicly? Will you journal? Will you spend time daily praising God and thanking Him for the freedom that is now yours? There are so many ways to thank Him for all He has done. Why not get started right away?

*Father, first of all I just want to pause and thank You—
from the bottom of my heart—for setting me free.
You've given me a new opportunity to come out from behind
the wall of shame I had built for myself. I was getting
so tired of living that way, Lord. Freedom has been
awesome, and a little scary. It's my new normal, and I'm still
adjusting to it. Thank You for the sunlight of freedom.
Help me with each bold step I take, Father. Amen.*

The Battle for Perfection

Not that we are sufficient in ourselves to claim anything as coming from us, but our sufficiency is from God.
2 CORINTHIANS 3:5

. . . .

If you've ever seen the movie *Mary Poppins*, you know that Mary describes herself as "practically perfect in every way." It seems as if she believes it too! But of course no one is perfect, not even Mary. We're all flawed and in need of Christ's redemption.

But stop to think about that phrase for a minute. Is that what you expect of yourself. . .perfection? Are you a perfectionist? Are you harder on yourself than others are on you? Are the demands you place on yourself impossible to meet? Do you work overtime trying to reach goals that are simply unreachable or unsustainable?

Many perfectionists struggle with feeling like they never quite measure up, no matter how hard they try. In their mind's eye, they're good. . .but not good enough. And nothing they'll ever do will quite make the mark.

Sound familiar? If so, you might be a perfectionist. That 95 you got on the test? It should have been a 100. That speech you gave in class? You could have done better. That slice of cheesecake you ate after dinner? You should have chosen an apple or low-fat yogurt. You've been beating yourself up over it for hours and the shame just won't leave you alone.

Yep, you're a perfectionist.

Maybe it's time to ask this question: "Why am I so hard on myself? What makes me feel like I have to be perfect? Does this go back to my childhood, something I was taught while growing up? Or have I put this on myself?" Getting to the answer might take some time, but you can do it. Remember, God extends grace upon grace. We can never be perfect. Our sufficiency, as this verse states so beautifully, is from God. He fills in the gap between imperfect (us) and perfect (Him). Grace rides the line between those two.

So rest easy. No need for "practically perfect in every way" here. In Him, you are more than enough.

Father, I'm never going to be perfect, at least not until I get to heaven. That's why I need You so much. I'm grateful for Your grace, Lord. How can I ever thank You for bridging the gap between my imperfections and Your holiness? I stand in awe of You, Lord. Amen.

Sprinkled Clean

*When a Samaritan woman came to draw water, Jesus said
to her, "Will you give me a drink?" (His disciples had gone
into the town to buy food.) The Samaritan woman said to him,
"You are a Jew and I am a Samaritan woman. How can you ask
me for a drink?" (For Jews do not associate with Samaritans.)*
JOHN 4:7–9 NIV

"Will you give me a drink?"

Just six words, but they stopped the Samaritan woman in her
tracks. She stared at the stranger—gazed into that welcoming
face—and shook her head. "How is it that you, a Jew, ask a drink
of me, a woman of Samaria?" Such a thing was impossible to
fathom. Jews and Samaritans didn't speak to each other, after all.

What happened next threw her off guard and nearly caused
her to drop her water jar. He stared at her with such compassion
in those amazing eyes that her heart jolted within her.

"If you knew who it was asking for the drink," He said, "you
would have asked for living water."

"Wh–what?" These words confused her even more. Living
water? What in the world was that? She'd never heard of such a
thing, not from any of the locals, anyway.

"Everyone who drinks this water"—the stranger gestured to
the well—"will grow thirsty again. But if you drink the water I give,

you will never be thirsty again."

The woman's entire perspective changed in that very moment as she contemplated His words. "Sir," she said, "I'll have whatever You're drinking!"

Jesus offered the woman at the well eternal water from a well that would never run dry. He offers you the very same thing. Instead of running after things that satisfy only temporarily—relationships, food, alcohol, drugs—run to the One who offers water that satisfies eternally.

As you drink from that well, as you spend time with the Savior, you will discover a completely different way to live. No longer filled with shame, regret, or anguish, you'll have abundant life. And like the woman at the well, you will come to understand a Savior who loves you no matter where you've come from or what your current situation might be.

Now, that's a lovely cup of water!

Father, I want abundant life. I want the kind of water that causes me to stop thirsting after the temporary things of this world. Today I say, "I'll have whatever You're drinking, Lord!" Amen.

Picture Perfect: The Social Media Mama

For we all stumble in many ways. And if anyone does not stumble in what he says, he is a perfect man, able also to bridle his whole body.

JAMES 3:2

She's practically perfect in every way, that social media mama. She throws the best birthday parties for her children, keeps a tidy, organized house, always looks like a million bucks, and has a husband who makes other women envious. Her figure is perfect, her clothes are gorgeous, her skin looks great, she takes amazing vacations, she whips up the healthiest snacks for her kids, and she has all the best advice on how to maintain a perfect family.

Only one problem. . .it's all an illusion. In between snapshots of her practically perfect life, she's a wreck, but too ashamed to admit it. Because she's managed to convince the world that she lacks nothing, she finds it difficult to be vulnerable, to reach out to friends and loved ones with the truth of what's really going on in her world. So she suffers in silence, still posting pictures that provoke envy among her friends, all in an attempt to present a reality that simply isn't real.

No one is perfect. Beneath the shiny exteriors, there are warts, moles, bad attitudes, broken marriages, kids on drugs, repossessions, heartbreak, and much more. You can't see it through the perfectly placed smiles, but problems do exist, even for the ones who claim to have it all together.

What can be done to get past the facade? How can you help friends with a picture-perfect image? Start by being real in front of them. If you're struggling, admit it, even in front of those who appear "perfect." If you're in need of prayer, ask for it. If your kids aren't doing well in school or are struggling to fit in, don't be afraid to voice the truth. As soon as one person comes clean, the rest will follow.

We need each other too much to be fake. So toss the air-brushed photos. Get rid of the practically perfect facade and get real with those around you so that you can make a difference to hurting people. In the process, you will find freedom as well.

Father, I want to be real and vulnerable so that others feel encouraged to be the same. No more illusions of perfection from me, Lord. I'm going to let others see my imperfections so that they feel safe sharing their own. Amen.

The Ministry of Reconciliation

All this is from God, who through Christ reconciled us to himself and gave us the ministry of reconciliation.

2 CORINTHIANS 5:18

. . . .

"Even if I have to die with You, I will never disown You." Peter's words were laced with passion and determination. How could Jesus think that he, one of Christ's most faithful disciples, might be capable of turning on Him? The very idea repulsed Peter. He would sooner give up his own life than deny his Savior, his friend. Impossible!

And yet a short time later, when confronted by Jesus' accusers, that's exactly what he did. Peter denied Jesus not once, but three times. Can you even imagine such an abrupt change of heart? Surely fear prompted him to let those awful words slip out. And the shame that followed must have stopped him in his tracks. Would his betrayal separate him from his friend forever, or could he somehow make the relationship right again?

Jesus, in His mercy, gave Peter three opportunities to redeem himself—not just to say the right thing, but to do the right thing. With those words "Lord, You know I love You," Peter redeemed himself. Had he chosen to remain in his shame, he might never have gone on to impact the early church the way he did. Instead, he stepped out of darkness and into the light of forgiveness.

God had big plans for Peter's life, things he couldn't yet see when those denials were fresh on his lips. And God has big plans for you too. Sure, you've failed in the past. You've said things—and done things—you wish you hadn't. You've even turned your back on your faith a time or two. You've had regrets, buckets full. But Jesus sees past all of that and looks to your heart. He's ready to offer second chances. . .and third. . .and fourth.

Don't let your yesterdays define your tomorrows. Follow Peter's lead. Look your Savior in the eye, place your hand in His, and take steps forward, not back. He has great plans for you no matter where you've come from. It's where you're headed that matters most to the Lord. Right now, head straight into His arms.

Father, I want to run to You with clean hands and a pure heart, undefiled by this world. But I know I'm not perfect. I've failed You so many times. Thank You for pouring out forgiveness, even when I know I don't deserve it. I'm so grateful for Your grace and for second chances, Father. Amen.

The Lifter of My Head

But you, O LORD, are a shield about me,
my glory, and the lifter of my head.
PSALM 3:3

. . . .

Traci couldn't help but cry when her neighbor made the announcement that a baby was on the way. How could she manage all of the conflicting emotions battling inside of her right now?

Sure, celebrating with her friend was important, but why had God chosen to give a child to someone else. . .and not to her? Again. Would she ever carry a baby in her arms, or would this hole in her heart deepen with every friend's announcement? Was she destined to remain childless forever?

With head held high, Traci persevered. She attended the baby shower, showed up at the hospital with flowers, even stopped by her neighbor's house to welcome the little one after his arrival. All with a smile on her face. She did her best to mask her personal pain and offer plenty of smiles and coos as she held her friend's little one. And why not? Babies are worth smiling about.

But inside, the usual twisting in her heart made the smile seem forced. She longed for a child of her own. She wanted what all new moms have—tiny giggles, little toes to nibble, chubby tummies to tickle. She wanted dirty diapers, late-night crying sessions, and laundry baskets filled with onesies.

She wanted a baby. And the fact that she hadn't had one yet ate at her like a cancer. Would she ever get past these feelings? Would God give her the child she prayed for?

Perhaps you've walked a mile in this woman's shoes. Maybe you wondered (are even wondering now) if you would ever have a child to love. Perhaps you're ashamed of how you feel when you receive news that a friend is expecting. But you can't seem to help yourself.

God sees your struggles, and He cares. He knows your greatest longings and has already put plans in motion for how to meet your deepest needs. So settle back in His care. Free your heart to celebrate with those around you in preparation for the joys that are yet to come.

Father, I want what I don't yet have, and it's been eating away at me. I confess that I'm not just jealous; I'm hurting. Terribly. Father, please forgive me for the attitude I've adopted. I want to be set free, Lord, so that I'm ready when my time comes. I trust You, Lord. Amen.

No More Hiding

*And he said, "I heard the sound of you in the garden,
and I was afraid, because I was naked, and I hid myself."*
GENESIS 3:10

. . . .

She refused to divulge the name of her child's father. Instead, Hester Prynne, a young Puritan woman, took the shame and blame of bearing her daughter, Pearl, out of wedlock on her own. She wore the scarlet *A* on her breast wherever she went, a sign to all that she was a sinner, an adulterer. The crowd ridiculed, jeered, even ostracized her. Shame permeated her very being. Others thrust it upon her, and she could not shake it, no matter how hard she tried.

An outcast from society, Hester did her best to live her life and function as normal for the sake of her child. Even as Pearl grew older, Hester attempted to provide a normal life so that her daughter wouldn't have to carry her mother's shame. It wasn't the child's fault, after all, though she seemed to bear the brunt of her parents' mistakes.

Somewhere out there, a man carried shame as well, but his was seared on the heart. The father of Hester's daughter kept his secret buried deep. Through many years of self-torture and inner wrangling, Reverend Dimmesdale's secret remained intact. . .until he just couldn't take it anymore. The dam broke wide and all was revealed.

That's what guilt will do to you. It eats away at the core of you until you're barely able to function anymore. In Dimmesdale's case, it ended in his untimely demise.

God never intended for us to live with deep-seated regrets like that. He offers a way out through His Son, Jesus. When we accept His forgiveness, His work on the cross, we can lay down our guilt and shame and be set free. Jesus can remove the scarlet letter from your chest today, if you let Him. Run to Him. Let Him offer you the great exchange—His life for yours. Your story will truly have a happy ending if you hand over all your regrets to the One who stands ready to take them once and for all.

Father, I've lived with deep regrets and shame for things I've done in secret. Like Reverend Dimmesdale, I've hidden away things that I'm not proud of. Today I expose all my shortcomings and sins to You. I ask for Your forgiveness, Your grace, and Your salvation. I turn from my past and ask You to cleanse this scarlet stain, now and forever. Amen.

Take Every Thought Captive

For though we walk in the flesh, we are not waging war according to the flesh. For the weapons of our warfare are not of the flesh but have divine power to destroy strongholds. We destroy arguments and every lofty opinion raised against the knowledge of God, and take every thought captive to obey Christ.
2 CORINTHIANS 10:3–5

Sharon stared at her reflection in the mirror and groaned. Try as she might, she couldn't force her smile to cover the crooked teeth. She made multiple attempts, but every smile looked forced. If only her parents could have afforded braces when she was younger. That would have fixed everything. Well, not everything. She was riddled with flaws, after all. The issues went far beyond her crooked teeth or odd smile.

Take that tummy, for instance! Why was it poking out? Had she really put on weight? Maybe if she sucked it in, no one would notice. Then again, a strained smile and sucked-in belly probably wouldn't look very natural. Maybe she should just forget about her flaws and be herself. If only she could do that without fretting. Wouldn't that be wonderful?

Perhaps you understand this woman's concerns. You have flaws too. Your ears are too big. You don't like your nose. You've got crinkles around your eyes. Your thighs rub together. Your ankles are fat. On and on the list goes. And the mirror does little to calm your anxieties. In fact, it exaggerates them. For in that glass you see all that you were afraid you'd see. . .and it only makes you more depressed.

As you examine who you are (physically speaking), remember that God created you with those ears, that nose, those ankles. He's not ashamed of His creation. You are His workmanship, created in His image. He doesn't look down at you and say, "That one really embarrasses Me." On the contrary, He sings and dances over you, celebrating every fine detail, including your freckles and moles. There's nothing about your physical anatomy that shocks Him. So stop fretting over your imperfections. Begin to celebrate the body that God gave you.

Father, I might not be perfect, but You adore me.
Have I mentioned how grateful I am for that? Thank You
for teaching me how to take every thought captive so
that I'm no longer bound to my feelings, Lord. Amen.

A New Day Dawning

The LORD within her is righteous; he does no injustice;
every morning he shows forth his justice; each dawn
he does not fail; but the unjust knows no shame.
ZEPHANIAH 3:5

It's a strange phenomenon, is it not? Those who *shouldn't* feel shame often do, and those who *should* feel shame for their actions (or at the very least should suffer pangs of conscience for their horrific actions) often do not.

Why is that? Why are some people more apt to take on shame than others? Does their shame meter need a reset? And what's up with those people who never seem to feel guilty about anything? Don't they have a conscience at all?

We're all unique and deal with emotional and psychological situations differently. Some of us were taught to carry shame by our parents, who led by example or who inflicted shame on us as children. Others were raised by parents who felt like the rules didn't apply to them or that they were somehow entitled. These factors play a role in how we respond internally when we've done something wrong. And then there are those rare people who don't seem to have any meter at all. They do what they want, when they want, and to whom they want. They're so lost that they don't feel regret even under the most extreme circumstances.

But here's the truth: Only God can see the heart. He can reset the meter only when you come into relationship with Him. Even the vilest person, the one with no conscience at all, can have an encounter with the King of Kings and Lord of Lords. Even that person can walk in newness of life, free from the past.

From the point of conversion on, the Holy Spirit will do His work, pricking your conscience when necessary and cleansing you from guilt and despair. He longs to enter a full relationship with you. When you're in relationship with Jesus, when the Holy Spirit resides inside of you, the meter works perfectly. You don't even have to think about it, in fact. So pray for those around you, that they will come to know Christ. This is truly the only way they will ever come to grips with their actions. And trust that God is doing His perfect work—in their lives and in your own.

Father, I get it. Your Holy Spirit is my meter. Thank You for the eternal reset, Lord. There are so many people in my world who need You. I pray they will come to know You so that they can experience the joy of Your salvation and the added benefit of knowing how to respond to life's situations. Amen.

Wisdom for the Humble

When pride comes, then comes disgrace,
but with the humble is wisdom.
PROVERBS 11:2

. . . .

Little Carter never meant to grow up without a father. If he had his way, a proud dad would show up for every ball game, cheering him on, camera in hand. He'd snap a million photos and upload them to social media so that everyone could see his amazing son hit a home run.

But that's not Carter's reality. Instead, he does the best he can to smile and cheer up his mom. She's been great since Dad left, in spite of everything. She always makes him feel special. Still, there's that longing deep in his soul for a dad, and he wonders if his dreams of a perfect family will ever come true.

When the other kids brag about special outings with their fathers or cool vacations, Carter doesn't say much. He sits quietly, taking it all in. Maybe one day he'll have a life like that. Until then, he keeps to himself when the kids start talking about their families. It's not his fault he doesn't have a dad, but he still ends up feeling ashamed of the fact. Still, what can he do, other than pray for a miracle?

Maybe you can relate to Carter. Maybe you grew up without a dad. . .or a mom. Maybe your dad was in and out of the picture, showing up for you at times, then disappearing into the shadows. You got your hopes up, only to have them dashed all over again. Disappointment rose up inside of you and you learned not to hope at all. After a while, you simply stopped talking or thinking about your unmet desires.

Here's one thing you need to know: it's not your fault. No child has ever been responsible for his or her parents' poor choices. Nothing you did—or didn't do—caused the situation around you. Rest in the knowledge of that truth, but learn from your experience too. What you lacked as a child you can provide as an adult.

No matter where you've come from, no matter what situation you grew up in, God can redeem the time. He can also train you how to become a great parent yourself so that the cycle ends with you. What the enemy meant for evil God can and will use for good, if you let Him.

Lord, thank You for the reminder that You can redeem time. Nothing is lost with You. No matter how difficult the situation, no matter how alone I've felt at times, You can bring something good from it. I'm counting on that, Father. Amen.

Desire Fulfilled

Hope deferred makes the heart sick,
but a desire fulfilled is a tree of life.
PROVERBS 13:12

. . . .

Think back to your childhood. Were you that kid who was invincible, afraid of nothing? Maybe you looked every foe directly in the eye, ready to do battle. Your fists were always up and ready, should an instigator start trouble. You would take him down, no problem. Just watch you!

Or were you the one hiding in the shadows, terrified even to put your foot in the shallow end of the pool? Maybe the others called you a scaredy-cat, a label you agreed with, both then and now. You wore it like an identity card and knew in your heart that you'd always live in fear of life.

The truth is our childhood experiences play a major role in our adult formation. If you spent your early years swallowed up by fear, terrified of every opportunity that came your way, you still might be suffering from fear today. It's hard to break old habits, after all. Your fear can affect everything—your ability to make presentations at work, your unwillingness to stand up for yourself against a cruel friend or boss. Literally every aspect of your adult life can be impacted by issues that were never resolved in childhood.

God never intended for you to live in fear. He gave you power, love, and a sound mind. . .for a reason. His desire is for you to step out in faith, to lift that chin, square those shoulders, and bravely face whatever challenges lie in front of you. And remember, when you are at your weakest, He remains strong. You're not walking this road alone. His hand is right there to lead you on.

There's no reason to feel shame that you're not a dynamo. Instead, let God build you from the inside out into a bolder, braver person so that you can thrive in this life. Lean on Him. Trust His strength, not your own. Together, with your hand in His, you really will be a force to be reckoned with.

Father, I want to be a spiritual dynamo, but I'm learning that You're the One with the power, not me. What a huge relief. I don't have to summon up courage because everything I am— everything I need—comes from You. I praise You for holding my hand and leading me forward, Lord. Amen.

Access with Confidence

In whom we have boldness and access with
confidence through our faith in him.
EPHESIANS 3:12

She probably never expected to find a husband at all, let alone a faithful one. But Gomer, accustomed to life on the streets, settled in with Hosea, the man God sent to rescue her from a fallen existence. From prostitute to housewife. What a jump! No doubt she found herself mesmerized by her great fortune in life. Sure, the neighbors talked. She expected that. But she would ignore them and get on with the business of adapting to her new normal.

For a while, Gomer handled married life well. Then, over time, she began to slip. The streets kept calling her back. She fought the temptation as long as she could, but old habits die hard. So back she went—to her former life, the men who abused her, a life of shame. She went back to old customs, old friends, old ways of functioning. She swapped the ideal for the lesser. . .and paid a heavy price.

Hosea, her faithful groom, never gave up. He followed closely behind, praying, hoping, believing she would return to him, a contented bride once more. But Gomer settled deeper and deeper into her lifestyle, a broken woman. Even an illegitimate child didn't stop her from sinking deeper in sin.

It took a lot of time and considerable persistence from Hosea, but he finally won her heart once more. He convinced her that she was worthy of his love, that nothing she could ever do would separate her from his affections.

Completely repentant, Gomer came home once again, a bride in need of a husband with a child in need of a father. No doubt she faced many regrets, but her husband continued to win her over with his great love.

Gomer's story is one we all can relate to. God woos us, wins our hearts, and brings us to dwell with Him. But we're torn. Old temptations nag at us until we finally relent. The Lord never gives up. He searches and searches, calls and calls, pleads with us to turn from our sin and shame and return to dwell with Him.

What a generous and loving God we serve. How He adores us!

Father, I'm more like Gomer than I care to admit. I keep slipping back into the patterns of my old life. Old habits die hard, even when I do my best. But You've won my heart, Lord. I don't want anything but You. May I never turn back, Father. Amen.

The Strength of My Heart

My flesh and my heart may fail, but God is the strength
of my heart and my portion forever.
PSALM 73:26

. . . .

If you were to make a list of the most famous missionaries in Christian history, Jim and Elisabeth Elliot would be high on the list. In 1956, while attempting to evangelize the Huaorani people of Ecuador, Jim (along with four other missionaries on his team) was murdered. His story captivated the world and caused deep anguish among other missionary workers and believers alike. No one could believe the shocking story. It seemed impossible.

No one would have blamed Elisabeth if she had given up on her work among the Huaorani and returned to the States with her young daughter, just ten months old. In fact, there were surely those who insisted she return home, for her own safety and well-being.

However, Elisabeth decided to stay on in Ecuador to fulfill the call on her life. She would pick up where Jim left off, and she would do so with God's blessing and power. Determined to make good of a tragic situation, she ended up returning to the very people who had taken her husband's life. Elisabeth evangelized the tribe, winning many to the Lord. In the end, she even befriended the very man who took her husband's life. Can you even imagine the shame he must have felt for the deaths he had caused?

Many would hear this story and wonder how—or why—Elisabeth chose to stay. They might also question her ability to face the people responsible for her husband's death—to forgive them and to enter into relationship with them. Somehow, she was able to see beyond what they had done to their souls in need of saving.

People have hurt you too. They've done things that some would call unforgivable. But if your heart is tender, like Elisabeth Elliot's, God can use you in remarkable ways. He can help you heal from the heartbreak and offer forgiveness, that others might come to know Him. He will be the strength of your heart, if you allow Him to be.

Lord, I don't know how Elisabeth did it, but I want to follow her lead. You were the strength of her heart, and I ask You to be the strength of mine as well. Help me as I forgive and move forward, I pray. Amen.

A Refuge for the Oppressed

The Lord is a refuge for the oppressed,
a stronghold in times of trouble.
PSALM 9:9 NIV

. . . .

He worked with every ounce of strength in him to save his patient, but he could not. The exhausted surgeon left the operating theater a broken man, twisted and torn from the inside out. Relaying the awful news to the family was just one more knife in his heart, but it was a task that could not be avoided. They fell apart on him, devastated to receive the news that the one they loved had passed away. Wasn't this supposed to have been a simple operation? How could something like this have happened? Had someone made a mistake?

No matter how many times he revisited the situation in his mind over the following weeks and months, the doubt still ate at him. Had he slipped up in some way? Made some sort of subtle mistake to cause this outcome?

No, the more he replayed the tapes in his head, the more convinced he was—he'd done nothing wrong. Every care had been taken. It was simply this patient's time to go.

So why did he bear it like a cross, as if he had caused this loss? Would he ever get past the nagging guilt that things should have ended differently? And how could he handle the incoming lawsuit, which blamed him for the death? Would it destroy his reputation, his very calling? Or would he somehow get past all of this to operate again?

Perhaps you can relate to this doctor's inner turmoil. Maybe you've felt unnecessary guilt after an accident or incident that you didn't cause. The feeling that you're to blame won't go away. God wants to ease your mind and bear your burden. Though it sounds cliché, He longs for you to release it from your hands and place it in His. You aren't big enough or strong enough to hold it anyway.

Circle today's date on the calendar so that you never forget: "This was the day I gave it to Jesus once and for all." Then release your burden to the Lord and never look back.

It's been so hard, Lord. I've lived with guilt that has left me in knots. I can't go back and undo the past, but I can move forward. Please take the pain and turmoil, I pray. I give it to You today. Amen.

An Anchor of the Soul

*We have this as a sure and steadfast anchor of the soul,
a hope that enters into the inner place behind the curtain.*

HEBREWS 6:19

. . . .

The sailor held tight to the ropes that controlled the sails while the wind knocked his small wooden boat this way and that. All around him, waves crashed and roared, threatening to take his vessel down to the depths of the sea. He tilted to the right and then the left as massive waves caused water to fill the boat. Was this really the way his story was destined to end?

Panic rose in his chest. It seemed like the storm would never end. At times he felt sure he would die before seeing land again. Then, from out of nowhere, the waves calmed. The boat steadied. The sailor drew in a deep breath and prayed the worst was behind him. Maybe he would see dry land again after all. With newfound hope, he grabbed the ropes and attempted to steer toward shore once again.

Maybe you've been in a situation that felt like that. Everything around you was swirling and toppling and all sense of control was lost. You attempted to adjust the proverbial sails, but nothing helped. Water filled your boat and you felt a sense of impending doom. You were going under, and soon.

And then, from out of nowhere, total peace overtook you.

Everything changed as you found yourself trusting in Jesus. He somehow calmed your heart, even when everything around you was still spinning out of control.

Here's the truth: in the very middle of the storm, while the winds are threatening to take you down, God is there, a solid anchor, holding you steady. It might seem impossible—as you face the death of a loved one, a major illness, or a job crisis—but God can supernaturally intervene in even the hardest situation and bring peace. No matter where you are, no matter what you're walking through, invite Him into your situation. He longs to be an anchor for your soul so that you will pull through.

Father, thank You for being my anchor. I feel like the wind is tearing me to pieces, but You're right there, steadying me and giving me supernatural peace. I don't understand it, Father, but I'm so grateful for it. Thank You, my Peacemaker! Amen.

Let's Reason It Out

"Come now, let us reason together, says the LORD:
though your sins are like scarlet, they shall be as white as snow;
though they are red like crimson, they shall become like wool."
ISAIAH 1:18

. . . .

This passage from Isaiah is quite an eye-opener, isn't it? Can you imagine sitting across the table from the King of Kings, coffee cup in hand, to reason things out? You have a lot on your mind, and so does He. You give Him your opinion; He gives you His. You share your frustrations; He quiets the storm going on inside of you. You let Him know your struggles; He offers fresh, workable answers. You point the finger over a situation that seems unfair; He responds with pure affection and comfort. Nothing you say offends or upsets Him. He seems to take it all in stride, never losing the look of love and compassion in His eyes. Wow, what a conversation!

We don't always understand the ways of the Lord. Many times, we point to the heavens and shout, "Why me, Lord?" or "I don't get it! I've been doing all the right things." When it comes right down to it, we aren't meant to fully understand the mind of God. Adam and Eve had the same dilemma. They wanted God knowledge but couldn't pay the price tag associated with it.

What do you need to reason out today? Are you knotted up

about something? Is a relationship in turmoil, a job in trouble, a teen behaving badly? You can talk these things out with God.

Whether you've been cheated out of something by someone you trusted or you're struggling to get the bills paid, the Lord is right there, ready to share His heart with you. He's not angry or unapproachable. He adores you and wants you to ask the "Why?" questions. You might not understand His timetable or His way of leading you to the answers, but eventually all things will become clear. Until then, grab that cup of coffee and meet with Him for a lengthy chat.

Lord, can we sit awhile and talk? I need to get to the bottom of some things. I need Your perspective. I also need time to share my heart, to get a few things off my mind. Thank You for listening, and for speaking. I'm grateful for Your willingness to reason things out with me. Amen.

Full Assurance

Let us draw near with a true heart in full assurance of faith,
with our hearts sprinkled clean from an evil conscience
and our bodies washed with pure water.
HEBREWS 10:22

. . . .

Zealous, angry, ready to do business with anyone who might associate himself with Christ, Saul traveled down the road to Damascus. His thoughts were in turmoil as he contemplated the recent stoning of a young Christ follower named Stephen, a strange fellow with a contented look in his eyes as he gave his life willingly for the cause of Jesus Christ. Where did these radical believers get their strange notions, anyway? What made them so passionate, so dedicated? Why would they be willing to give their very lives for the cause of a simple man? A heretic, no less. It made no sense to Saul whatsoever.

Then from out of nowhere, the sky lit in a shocking and dazzling display. Saul found himself blinded by the light and fell to his knees, overcome. What in the world was happening here?

A voice spoke from on high, "Saul, Saul, why do you persecute Me?"

God Almighty.

Stopped in his tracks, Saul could barely gather his thoughts. Why would God's first words be an accusation? Hadn't he, Saul, been a devout Jew, a pillar of the faith? Didn't God see that?

Completely blinded, Saul listened and obeyed all that he heard, and in doing so he changed the trajectory of his life forever. No longer a persecutor of Christians, he now found himself on their side as his radical conversion to the Christian faith took place.

Unfortunately, fellow believers didn't quite believe he'd made the switch. You can't blame them for not trusting the man who had just served as an accomplice to Stephen's stoning, after all. Many attempted to ostracize him and make him feel ashamed of who he had been. They simply didn't trust him.

Have you walked a mile in Saul's shoes? Have you come to a new belief in Christ, only to be ostracized by other believers because of your former life? Don't get angry. God will prove all that needs to be proven as you live your life before them in a way that honors Him.

Lord, I haven't always been made to feel welcome.
Some people don't like who I used to be, where I came from.
But You're giving me the patience I need, Father. My life
will be all the proof they need. In the meantime, I'll try to
remember that it's Your opinion that matters anyway,
not the opinions of other people. Amen.

Remembered No More

*"For I will be merciful toward their iniquities,
and I will remember their sins no more."*
HEBREWS 8:12

. . . .

Remember those old soap operas, the ones with unbelievably colorful characters who suffered from strange and perplexing diagnoses like amnesia? The storylines were good for a laugh back in the old days, weren't they? You didn't really believe the character could have forgotten his past, but it made for good fiction. And it kept the storyline going for weeks, months, and even years to come. If the character could claim amnesia, any number of plotlines could be drawn out.

Here's an amazing truth: God chooses to have amnesia when it comes to your sin. He deliberately remembers to forget. (How's that for a fun twist?) He tosses that sin as far as the east is from the west and remembers it no more. And "no more" means, well, no more. He simply can't remember it. He's decided not to.

Think about that for a moment. That's a lot of effort for God to go to. The God of all creation—the One who made the heavens and the earth, the One who knows all—makes a *choice* to forget.

And He longs for you to forget the sins of yesterday too, because He knows the consequences of hanging on. Too many believers are unnecessarily haunted by memories of the past.

They need to be set free for good.

Today, ask the Lord to show you how to forget. . .as He forgets. This is His desire for you, after all. Ask for sin amnesia. Ask for shame amnesia. Ask for the supernatural ability to put your former deeds behind you. It will be better than the storyline of an old TV show, for sure, because God's version of amnesia will free you up to live a happier, healthier life, completely unencumbered. Your plotline will take you straight into the arms of the One who loves you most and cares for you above all.

What's holding you back today? Let it go, then remember to forget!

Father, I want to forget. I don't like to be haunted by things I once did. Today I'm asking for shame amnesia. Wash away any remembrance, I pray. Help me to let go of the past once and for all, along with all shameful memories associated with it. Amen.

Abide

By this we know that we abide in him and he in us,
because he has given us of his Spirit.
1 John 4:13

. . . .

Most canines are perfectly content to lie at their master's feet (or side) for hours on end. When the master moves, the pup moves with him. When one sits, the other sits. When one eats, the other wants to eat. They are two peas in a pod, moving in perfect unison and resting comfortably with each other.

Why do canines experience this kind of contentment? Why are they drawn to one master in particular? Why don't they ever get bored or move on to someone else instead?

Dogs have an innate ability to abide. They're content to just "be" with their masters. No agenda. No rushing about. No special days at the park necessary. To curl up at the master's side is plenty to keep that precious pooch content. They abide because they trust. They trust because time has proven the master trustworthy.

We have a lot to learn from canines, don't we? It's so hard for us to sit still, to commune with God. Instead of abiding, we want to be on the run—completely off leash. Instead of being, we're all about doing. We sometimes yearn for other masters. . .or no master at all.

If you look up synonyms for the word *abide*, you'll find a few of the following: *obey, observe, follow, keep to, stick to, stand by, act in accordance with.* When you're comfortable in God's presence, you're willing to "stick to" Him, to stand by Him. Your actions are all in accordance with who He is. The reason you're so comfortable "keeping to" Him is because you know His presence is the safest place to be. You abide because you trust. You trust because you know He's got your back, in good times and bad. In many ways, you're like that canine, completely content to sit at your Master's feet.

What's keeping you from abiding today? Have you allowed shame to separate you from your Master? Never be afraid to draw close, to sit at His feet. Don't allow lingering issues to pull you away. He longs to spend time with you today, simply abiding.

I want to abide with You, Father. No running. No tugging. No pulling away. No chasing other masters. Today, I simply want to be with You, Lord, content at Your side. Amen.

Without Regret

For godly grief produces a repentance that leads to salvation without regret, whereas worldly grief produces death.
2 CORINTHIANS 7:10

. . . .

As a single mom, Bridget always did her best. In fact, other parents looked to her as an example of what single motherhood should look like. Bridget had her act together. Well, mostly.

If you asked her about what happened at the family's mealtimes, she would tell you that the kids didn't have the most nutritious foods on their plates. Whatever she could put together on a budget would have to do. While other kids carried healthy lunches to school, hers were lucky to have PB&J sandwiches or be on the school lunch program. While most moms cooked a nutritious dinner, she drove through the kids' favorite budget-friendly fast-food place night after night, ordering from their dollar menu. What else could she do? It was too late to cook, anyway.

She prayed her children would thrive, despite any lack, and always did her best, but the guilt ate away at her. When and how could she turn things around? Would she ever get past this stage? Sure, the kids should be more help. They could cook and clean. But she hadn't done the best job teaching them how to do that, had she? Regrets abounded.

Here's the truth: Not everyone has access to the best foods

or the best situations. There are families across this globe who barely make ends meet, who don't have the wherewithal to pull together a hot, home-cooked meal to be shared around a table. And many of those families—rushed, exhausted, broke—are barraged with images on social media of perfect parents who offer only the finest foods for little Joey or Susie, carefully and lovingly prepared by tender hands.

Maybe you fall somewhere in the middle. You try to offer good nutrition, but you're not always able to because of your crazy schedule. Deep breath, Mom. You're doing the best you can, and that's what matters. Eat the PB&J today. The hot meal can wait for tomorrow.

Lord, I want to do right by my kids, and that means taking proper care of their nutrition. Help me with this, I pray. I'm so overwhelmed that I can't seem to wrap my head around what needs to be done to get started. I'm open to Your ideas, Father. Amen.

He Lives in Me

*I have been crucified with Christ. It is no longer I who live,
but Christ who lives in me. And the life I now live
in the flesh I live by faith in the Son of God,
who loved me and gave himself for me.*

GALATIANS 2:20

. . . .

Whenever we do something wrong, we feel guilty. Our consciences are pricked. The Bible calls this conviction. The Holy Spirit convicts us of our sin, our poor choices. This conviction causes us to want to do better, to be better, to lean more heavily on Christ.

Shame has a different approach. Without our doing anything wrong at all, shame tries to tell us that we're innately flawed. Broken. Bad. Unworthy. Instead of pressing us closer to God, it nudges us away by convincing us we're not worthy of spending time in His presence.

But where do such accusations come from?

In many cases, we're taught these things as children by parents who don't know any better. In other cases, teachers, church leaders, or other well-meaning adults convince us we are bad and therefore unable to receive grace or love. These feelings can get twisted up inside of us and cause a lifetime of turmoil, resulting in separation from the people we love and from the Lord, who wants nothing more than for us to turn to Him with all of these struggles.

The truth is you're no more flawed than the next person. We all sin and fall short of the glory of God. That's why we need Him so much. Sure, you've struggled with beating yourself up. But here's good news: Every flaw, every broken place, was on Jesus' mind when He went to the cross on your behalf. He died to make broken people whole, to make the unloved feel loved, and to convince the bad that His goodness is enough. It's no longer you who lives—it's Christ in you.

Think about that for a moment. If Christ is living in you, how can you go on beating yourself up? He's right there, resident in your heart. To beat yourself up is to beat Him up.

It's time for a fresh perspective. The work of Christ is complete and lacking nothing. You are now living a life of faith. It's time to settle in and enjoy it!

Jesus, I've seen myself as flawed for so many years.
There have been times I thought I was beyond Your reach.
But You died for people just like me, and Your work on the
cross was complete. I commit to live by faith in You,
Lord. You've set me free from feelings of inadequacy,
Jesus, and I'm so grateful. Amen.

Perfect Love Casts Out Fear

There is no fear in love, but perfect love casts out fear.
For fear has to do with punishment, and whoever
fears has not been perfected in love.

1 John 4:18

She hid from the world in her home, unable to move outside its confines. Groceries were delivered. Meals were brought in. She ordered clothes and necessities online. Even the practical things like lightbulbs, toilet paper, and detergents were delivered to her door. All of this, in an attempt to remain in the one place she felt safe, her own home, apart from the rest of the world.

Her situation didn't start out like this. Once upon a time, she was a social butterfly. She thought nothing of being among people—strangers, friends, coworkers. . .didn't matter. She could handle them all with ease.

But then tragedy struck. It riveted her in place and made her unable to function in the normal ways. So she tucked herself away to protect herself from further pain. To be among people was just too difficult. It required too much of her. She couldn't handle the way she felt during those episodes, so they became fewer and farther between.

While this precious woman's situation might seem extreme to you, there are people who are genuinely afraid to step out of their comfort zone, so they isolate themselves even from those they love.

Perhaps on some lesser level you can relate. Maybe you're ashamed of your shyness or the fact that you're an introvert. Maybe you worry too much about what people think of you for not being bolder. Perhaps you've been given opportunities but turned them down out of fear. You just can't go there.

Even if you're completely locked in place, God has the key to unlock that door and set you free. It might take time. It might take help. But He can liberate you from the things that have you bound up—internally and externally. His perfect love truly can cast out any fear you might be facing.

What's holding you back today? What has you frozen in place? Ask God to begin the thawing process even now. There's a beautiful world out there, waiting for you to join in the song.

Father, I don't want to lock myself away from people anymore. I'm tired of being stuck in self-preservation mode. I want to be set free, Lord, to be among people again. I want to live a glorious life. Give me the courage and the strength, I pray. Amen.

Refiner's Fire

"I counsel you to buy from me gold refined by fire, so that you may be rich, and white garments so that you may clothe yourself and the shame of your nakedness may not be seen, and salve to anoint your eyes, so that you may see."
REVELATION 3:18

. . . .

Jonah found himself in the most precarious position ever when he refused to obey God. Swallowed up by a large fish, he had plenty of time to think about the actions—or lack thereof—that had led him here. How many times did he mumble the words "I should've gone to Nineveh!" while hanging out in the belly of that whale? Likely hundreds. Regrets abounded, to be sure. If he ever made it out of there alive, he'd never rebel against the Lord again.

That's one thing about feeling trapped. You have plenty of time to analyze and reanalyze all the things you should have done. Sure, you'll have regrets, but you'll also have an opportunity to do better next time.

Perhaps you've been caught up in a belly-of-the-whale scenario a time or two as well. Your actions led you to a place you never meant to go, where you felt trapped and alone, wishing you'd made a different choice. Even there, in that dark and gloomy place, it's not too late to reach out to God, to ask for His mercy and grace. In fact, He's pretty good at pulling people out of confining situations when they call out to Him. Just ask Jonah.

Those belly-of-the-whale moments often give us time to face our regrets and to do serious business with God over the times we've deliberately (or even inadvertently) strayed. In many ways, those seasons offer a time of refining in God's holy fire, a chance to be cleansed and set free. If we never went through the fire, we'd never be purified.

It's not too late. That's the message of Jonah's story. No matter how trapped you feel, no matter how much shame the enemy has heaped upon you. . .it's not too late. Allow God to do the refining required, then step out in freedom.

Father, I'm tired of being trapped. Today I confess that I've made mistakes. I've taken wrong turns. That's how I landed here, in this confined space. I repent, Lord. Please, do whatever refining work You see fit, then set me free so I can live fully for You. Amen.

Mighty to Save

"The LORD your God is in your midst, a mighty one who will save; he will rejoice over you with gladness; he will quiet you by his love; he will exult over you with loud singing."
ZEPHANIAH 3:17

. . . .

You wish there were more hours in a day. The pile of laundry taunts you, shaming you. A better mother would have that done by now. Dishes are stacked in the sink. You would deal with them, but the clean ones in the dishwasher haven't been emptied yet. You haven't found the time.

The messy garage beckons. Wouldn't it be great to park your car in there? If only you could slow down and take care of it. Your intentions are good, but you've been unable to make it happen. And what about that email inbox? It's never been this full. You have plans to respond to the most critical ones, but right now, even those will have to wait. More pressing matters are at hand—like working, sleeping, paying bills, and shoveling down a quick bite to eat before you start the cycle all over again.

Life is hectic. Frantic. At times, you don't know if you're coming or going. How you got in over your head, you're not sure, but the piles grow deeper with each passing day, and the prospect of dealing with them seems daunting. You're ashamed of yourself for stepping over them, but what else can you do? The promise of "Saturday's coming!" brings hope on the weekdays, but your weekends seem to be stolen away by an unforeseen enemy, intent on robbing you of sleep, rest, and organization.

God never intended for you to live at a frantic pace. To do so only brings regret over all the things that aren't being adequately taken care of. Deep breath. It's not too late. God is mighty to save! He can give you wisdom and instruction to ease your way out of this mess. Call on Him today. See His will, His way. Ask Him to intervene, to bring hope and order. He will guide you. . .if you let Him.

Father, I need You. Can You save me from this chaos? I feel like I'm drowning, Lord. I don't know how I'll ever get caught up. I need You now more than ever. Pull me from this wreckage, I pray, and help me set things right. Amen.

While We Were Yet Sinners

But God demonstrates his own love for us in this:
While we were still sinners, Christ died for us.

ROMANS 5:8 NIV

. . . .

Ebenezer Scrooge. Just the mention of his name sends a little shiver down the spine. That miserly old soul just couldn't seem to bring Christmas cheer to anyone, even himself. Sour-faced, stingy, mean, and alone, he brought doom and gloom wherever he went.

The name "Scrooge" continues to represent all who refuse to put others before themselves, all who place self over generosity. There are plenty of Scrooges across the globe, but God can reach those with even the hardest hearts and turn things around.

As Scrooge was led to his past, his present, and his future, he was riddled with shame and remorse, not just for his current actions, but particularly regarding the way they affected others.

There are many lessons to be learned from Scrooge's journey. Here's the best part of the story: while we are yet sinners, even in the middle of our shameful treatment of others, God still loves us. Jesus died for all the Scrooges of the world, whether they're young, middle-aged, or elderly.

Imagine this little ditty sung to the tune of "Jesus Loves the Little Children."

Jesus died for all the Scrooges,
all the Scrooges of the world.
Cold and nasty, rude and mean,
they're more precious than they seem.
Jesus died for all the Scrooges of the world.

It's true, you know. And if you happen to be a little on the Scrooge-ish side, remember, Jesus came to wipe away all traces of yesterday's sin, today's transgressions, and tomorrow's worries. Even now, while you're still a mess, Jesus stands ready to set you on the right path.

Father, I don't want to be known as a Scrooge. You have great things in store for me. I won't focus on yesterday. I won't worry about tomorrow. I'll live for today, with joy in my heart, ready to do good to others and to love You wholeheartedly. Amen.

Weep No More

And one of the elders said to me, "Weep no more; behold, the Lion of the tribe of Judah, the Root of David, has conquered, so that he can open the scroll and its seven seals."
REVELATION 5:5

. . . .

Stooped over the bedside of his dying child, King David was filled with remorse and shame. Had he not stolen another man's wife, had he not taken Bathsheba as his own, had he not arranged for that man to be killed in battle, none of this would have happened. Everything could have been prevented. . .if only. And now those "if onlys" were calling the shots.

David watched in anguish as his son took his last breath. Such agony, to lose a little one like this. The poor child had done nothing wrong, after all! Oh, if only David could go back and rewrite the story. Everything would end differently.

In spite of his pain, anguish, and guilt, David rose to face an uncertain future. How could he ever put these feelings of grief and despair behind him? Could God really give him a future when he'd caused so much pain for others?

Maybe you feel a kindredness with David. Maybe your sin has caused pain and grief for others. Maybe there were consequences. . .big consequences. Now you're wondering how—or if—God will redeem what's left of your life. You can't imagine it's possible, not after what you've done.

Here's some wonderful news. God went on to do amazing things in and through David. He wasn't defined by his sin with Bathsheba. With God's help, he managed to repent, dry his tears, and move forward to do remarkable things that influenced his generation and generations to come.

You can too. Even if you've caused unthinkable pain to others or yourself, you can begin again. There's still time to repent, to make things right. Restitution might be in order, but God will help you with that part too.

Weep no more. Better days are ahead.

Father, I've made mistakes. There's no denying that.
Many times I've had to pay a heavy price. On other occasions,
people I love have paid a price for my mistakes or decisions.
I'm genuinely sorry for those times, Lord. Please forgive me
and help me to move forward in a way that honors You
and those I've hurt. I want to have a hopeful future.
Please lead me there. Amen.

Shame Reinforcers

Bless the L ORD, O my soul, and forget not all his benefits,
who forgives all your iniquity, who heals all your
diseases, who redeems your life from the pit,
who crowns you with steadfast love and mercy.
PSALM 103:2–4

. . . .

Oh boy. Here she comes. That one person who's happy to make you feel guilty about yourself. She lives to reinforce your shame. You can hear her tongue clicking before she even gets close. She has a lot on her mind today, and you're about to hear all of it, whether you want to or not. And though she always delivers her messages with a smile on her face and condescension in her voice, her words are biting and hurtful. You can barely stand the way you feel about yourself when she's around.

So you turn and walk the other way. She might get her feelings hurt, but right now that's the least of your worries. You just need to protect yourself from her before she seeks to take you down once again. Getting away is the healthiest choice.

Do you struggle with people like this? Are any shame reinforcers ever-present in your life? Are they happy to remind you of the mistakes you've made, the times you've let them down? Do they belittle or injure you with their words?

There will always be shame reinforcers out there, but you

can protect yourself by not giving them space inside your head or heart. Instead, look for those who edify and uplift. You need Jesus friends, the ones who are happy to share the good they see in you.

Consider this verse from Psalm 103. If God redeems your life from the pit, if He's willing to crown you with steadfast love and mercy, why should your friends do otherwise? Are they greater than God? Should they have more say in your life? Of course not. So choose friends who speak life. Let me boldly proclaim over you that you are not who you once were, that you've come a long way, baby, and you're not turning back.

Father, show me how to avoid the shame reinforcers. I want to draw near to those who will encourage me as I step out in faith. I don't need continual reminders of who I used to be or how I messed up in the past. I'm looking ahead, not backward. Show me how to protect myself, I pray. Amen.

In Deed and in Truth

Little children, let us not love in word or talk but in deed and in truth. By this we shall know that we are of the truth and reassure our heart before him; for whenever our heart condemns us, God is greater than our heart, and he knows everything. Beloved, if our heart does not condemn us, we have confidence before God; and whatever we ask we receive from him, because we keep his commandments and do what pleases him.

1 JOHN 3:18–22

. . . .

Pimples. Chubby thighs. Academic problems. Peer pressure. Teens face a lot of challenges, don't they? They live in a world where everyone is expected to be perfect, and where they're made fun of—or shunned altogether—if they don't fit in. This is a tough time to be a teen.

As you think back on your teen years, which struggles bothered you the most? Were you shamed by others because you didn't look like them, dress like them, or have the same interests? Was your family at a different socioeconomic level, perhaps? Did you struggle to make the same grades or share the same talents? Comparison among teens is a real problem. Some teens are ostracized for their differences and looked down on if they have any flaws. But the reality is we're all flawed. No one is perfect, regardless of their social media headshot.

Perhaps you shiver as you think back on your teen years. Maybe they were tough. If you were left out because you weren't as popular, pretty, or smart as the other girls, then you know the sting of misplaced shame. It's tough feeling guilty for something you're not even guilty of, isn't it?

How can you make things better for the next generation? Look a teen squarely in the eye and say these words: "You're enough." That's what they need to hear, that they are enough. Love them in deed and in truth. Speak the Word over them. Let them know they have value. And if you see any misplaced shame in their lives, begin to come against it now, before it roots itself any deeper.

God can use you to reach a teen in your world. Who comes to your mind as you read that? Begin to pray for that teen even now. Then watch as God begins to use you. . .in deed and in truth.

Father, I want to be used to bring encouragement to teens and children in my world. There are so many people who feel on the fringes. Help me know what to say and do, I pray. Amen.

Stepping toward the Good

And we know that for those who love God all things work together for good, for those who are called according to his purpose.

ROMANS 8:28

. . . .

There's a rather infamous scene in *Little Women* where the spunky character Jo accidentally burns off her sister's hair using a hot curling iron. The girls are headed to a soiree at the home of a well-to-do neighbor, and Meg is mortified after her sister ruins her hair. They're already struggling to keep up with the Joneses because they don't have the proper wardrobe. Their gowns don't begin to compare to the ones worn by the other girls. And their shoes are out of style too. Now, missing hair? Talk about adding insult to injury. Meg can barely stand the idea that she still has to go, looking like this.

Perhaps this scene resonated with you like it has for so many others. It's hard not to feel ashamed when you're having trouble keeping up with the way other people dress or style their hair, the way they decorate their homes, or the kinds of people they socialize with. It can get to be a full-time job, just trying to be like everyone else.

That's why God isn't concerned with keeping up with the Joneses. He doesn't care if your hair is messy, your home isn't decorated to par, or your clothing isn't top of the line. He's not at all interested in whether your shoes are name brand or knockoffs. And He's not keen on you fretting over all those things either. There's no shame in being yourself. So what if your kitchen table is a hand-me-down? Who cares if your hair is pulled back in a ponytail? Why does it matter if your clothes came from the second-hand shop? Trends are ever-changing, anyway. By the time you buy new things, they're going out of style.

It's time to stop trying to keep up. Step away from that temptation and enjoy the freedom of just being you. You'll be happier for it.

Father, I'll admit, I care too much about what other people think of me—how I look, who I hang out with, where I live, what kind of car I drive. Today I step back from all of that and say, "No more." I want to be free to be myself, Lord. Help me, I pray. Amen.

Holy, Holy, Holy!

"You are worthy, our Lord and God, to receive glory and honor and power, for you created all things, and by your will they were created and have their being."

REVELATION 4:11 NIV

. . . .

What a glorious picture of heaven! Picture the twenty-four elders falling down before the King of all kings to shout praises at the top of their lungs. Can you hear it?

> *Day and night they never stop saying:*
> *"'Holy, holy, holy*
> *is the Lord God Almighty,'*
> *who was, and is, and is to come."*
> *Whenever the living creatures give glory, honor and thanks*
> *to him who sits on the throne and who lives for ever and ever,*
> *the twenty-four elders fall down before him who sits on*
> *the throne and worship him who lives for ever and*
> *ever. They lay their crowns before the throne and say:*
> *"You are worthy, our Lord and God,*
> *to receive glory and honor and power,*
> *for you created all things,*
> *and by your will they were created*
> *and have their being." (Revelation 4:8–11 NIV)*

When you picture this glorious scene, can you see yourself as part of the crowd, shouting and singing praises? All sins, washed away. All shame, a thing of the past. All regrets, washed by the blood. In the eternal presence of your Savior, only one thing remains on your lips, and that's praise to Him.

This is your future! This is how the story ends. One day you'll be in heaven, surrounded by millions—if not billions—of people (and angelic beings) who are lifting up the name of Jesus, all in one accord. Can you even begin to imagine what it will be like on that great day? It will be worth it all—every heartache, every bump in the road—just to be with Him forever.

Father, I can't wait! What an amazing picture of heaven. What a holy glimpse into eternity. I can hardly wait to spend time at Your throne, worshipping in spirit and in truth. And with all of the nations gathered around You, I'll hear worship as I've never heard before. It's going to be amazing, Lord, and I can't wait. Amen.

Not Dismayed

Fear not, for I am with you; be not dismayed, for I am your God; I will strengthen you, I will help you, I will uphold you with my righteous right hand.

ISAIAH 41:10

You did it. You summoned up the courage to step out, to join that committee at the church. And they welcomed you with open arms. At least, at first. Before long, you had all sorts of creative ideas flowing to improve the women's ministry or the children's department. You could hardly wait to share them with the team. You put together a plan, sketched it all out on paper, even brought notes to share with the others.

Unfortunately, your well-thought-out ideas fell on deaf ears. No one seemed to think they had any merit, from what you could glean from the yawns that followed your passionate discourse. And those papers you printed up? They got tossed to the side, as if they had no value at all.

So you clammed up. You closed your mouth and your heart. And though you didn't physically step away from the team, you closed off your thoughts and your heart to the possibility of joining in when others offered their ideas. What would be the point when they clearly didn't appreciate you? No, you'd just sit and listen, thank you very much. No point in letting them bring you down even further.

No doubt, this sort of encounter left its mark on you. You didn't set out to get your feelings hurt, but it happened. Now what? Do you go on with these feelings of inadequacy and embarrassment put on you by others, or do you move forward with a different group of friends in the hope that they will value your ideas?

First, God wants you to get past any lingering feelings of inadequacy that might be holding you down. He wants to remind you that your ideas have merit. Don't give up. Don't be dismayed. There will be other projects. There will be other teams. There will be people out there who see your worth. God will lead you to them, if you ask Him to. And while you're waiting, go ahead and forgive those who hurt you. You'll be freed up for the next task once you've released them back to the Lord.

Father, I need Your help finding the right teams to join. I want to be helpful, useful. I don't want to leave feeling like I'm not needed or wanted. Strengthen me, I pray, and guide me to the right place so that I can be of help to others. Amen.

Walk and Not Faint

*But those who hope in the L*ORD *will renew their strength.*
They will soar on wings like eagles; they will run and
not grow weary, they will walk and not be faint.
ISAIAH 40:31 NIV

. . . .

She bustled in the front door of the house, fast-food bags in hand. Her husband was working late. Again. The kids were old enough to fend for themselves, but they needed time with Mom and Dad too. She tossed the burger bags onto the kitchen table and called out for the kids to join her. They said quick hellos, gobbled down food, left a mess on the table, and headed to their rooms to do homework then get ready for bed. She barely had time to ask them about their days. Did her youngest look troubled about something? Her oldest seemed in a bad mood too. But when would she have the time to get to the bottom of things? Maybe she could make time this weekend.

No, they had that big company picnic this weekend. A quiet conversation with her son would have to wait. He would understand. She hoped.

She cleared the table, welcomed her husband home from work, then made her way to the shower, hoping it would help her clear her thoughts. The strain of the day caught up with her before she made it into the water, and she decided to skip the shower and go straight to bed. There would be plenty of time to bathe tomorrow morning. Before work.

Maybe you've known the exhaustion of this poor mom. Somewhere between marriage, kiddos, work, and housework, you're drowning in exhaustion. You can't keep up at work either, something that's really been troubling you. You're so overwhelmed with it all, but don't know how to stop the carousel from spinning.

It's time to hop off that un-merry-go-round and ask God to help you bring things into proper alignment. Before another day goes by, take a look at your schedule. . .a close look. Make sure you've carved out enough time for the Lord and for your family. Don't jump into one more project before you get your priorities straight. Ask God to help you. He's been right there all along, prompting you to do this very thing.

I'm ready to get off the carousel, Lord. I'm done with being exhausted and behind schedule. Please give me a proper plan to bring things into alignment, I pray, so that this never happens again. Amen.

A Crown of Righteousness

And now the prize awaits me—the crown of righteousness, which the Lord, the righteous Judge, will give me on the day of his return. And the prize is not just for me but for all who eagerly look forward to his appearing.

2 TIMOTHY 4:8 NLT

The father-daughter dance only came around once a year, but Allie didn't have a father to accompany her, so she was never able to attend. She tried to act like it didn't matter, but when her friends started posting pictures of themselves in their beautiful dresses, standing alongside their dads, something inside of her snapped.

"Why don't I have a dad who cares? Why can't he show up for something as important as this?"

Allie tried to squelch her feelings of anger and shame, but they would not be tamped down. Nothing about this was fair. Other girls had fathers. Other girls got to do fun things with their dads. Other girls got to shop for beautiful dresses and new shoes for the dance. They got dolled up and were treated like princesses. She had to sit at home and watch a movie with Mom. Again. Just like last year and the year before that.

Not that Mom was bad. No, in fact, she was being extra nice today. Maybe she understood what Allie was going through. She seemed a little sad too.

Still, the whole thing stunk. And it wasn't fair. Why couldn't her life just be normal?

Can you relate to Allie's feelings? Have you ever been excluded from an event because you somehow didn't meet the requirements? Maybe you found yourself on the outside looking in.

God never leaves you on the outside. With Him, you're always welcome. The only requirement for an eternal dance with Him is that you give Him your heart. You are His daughter, His princess. He has a crown of righteousness laid up for you, and it's not one you have to earn. It's one He gives freely.

Run to your Daddy-God's arms today. Let Him spin you around the dance floor. He will heal the broken places and convince you that He loves spending time with you.

Father, thank You for the reminder that You're my Daddy-God. I am precious in Your sight, loved by You. Thank You for making me feel so welcome. I give You my heart today. Amen.

A Clear Conscience

I thank God, whom I serve, as my ancestors did,
with a clear conscience, as night and day I
constantly remember you in my prayers.
2 TIMOTHY 1:3 NIV

. . . .

If you've read the classic short story *The Necklace*, you might recall the character Mathilde's deep anguish when she realizes she's lost an expensive diamond necklace she had borrowed from a friend, Madame Forestier. (Can you imagine losing something so expensive that belongs to someone else?)

In a panic, Mathilde goes to a nearby shop and finds a similar piece for 40,000 francs, far beyond what she can afford, but her only real option for redeeming the situation. She and her husband sell everything they own and take on loans with high interest rates in an attempt to cover the cost of the replacement necklace. They tell no one, of course, because the shame would do them in. Still, Mathilde can't help but realize—all of this has taken place because she was so worried about fitting in with her peers. Her pride got in the way and caused tremendous grief, not just for herself, but for her husband as well. Now there's a price to pay.

Mathilde's life disintegrates as she loses everything. The following years are spent slaving away to pay back the debt. More years go by. She is filled with regret over the deep loss, but what can she do? One day, Mathilde runs into Madame Forestier unexpectedly. Poor Mathilde is barely recognizable to her old friend. Heartbroken, Mathilde spills the story of what she's done. Imagine her shock when she learns that the necklace Madame Forestier had loaned to her all those years ago was nothing but a fake, made of paste.

This poor woman! She gave her entire life to ease her own conscience. Aren't you glad it isn't like that with God? No matter how badly we fail, He doesn't charge it to our account. He covers the debt, not just for now, but for all eternity. You can stand before Him with a clean conscience once you've accepted His free gift of salvation. You won't arrive at heaven's gate with a debt owing. The words "Paid in full!" are all you will ever hear.

How can I ever repay You, Lord? You've covered my debt in full. I've squandered so much of my life, but You've redeemed it, given me value. Thank You for wiping away every transgression, Father. Amen.

All Things

I know what it is to be in need, and I know what it is to have plenty. I have learned the secret of being content in any and every situation, whether well fed or hungry, whether living in plenty or in want. I can do all this through him who gives me strength.

PHILIPPIANS 4:12–13 NIV

After the stock market crash of 1929, the United States went through several years of deep economic and psychological depression. Individuals and families by the millions were affected. Many lost their land, their homes, their very livelihoods. Others lost their businesses, their jobs, their primary sources of income. For some who had been wealthy, this was a deep blow. For those who were already poor, it was devastating.

Adding insult to injury, many also lost their self-respect. They found it hard to maneuver through their new reality or to see the future as a hopeful place. In short, they gave up.

Have you ever been that low? Have you journeyed through a financial or psychological valley so deep that you wondered if you would ever see the light of day again? Has the word *depression* become more than a vague term to you during such rough seasons? Does despair rule your every thought when circumstances come against you? Have you taken on shame related to your situation, a situation that you did not cause?

God longs for you to be set free from misplaced shame. He knows what it's like to traverse low places. His Son carried the weight of the world on His shoulders that day He trudged toward Golgotha with the cross on His back. The situation must have felt unbearable to both Father and Son during that difficult journey to the hill where Jesus would offer His life. But He could see beyond the cross, to the millions of lives that would be transformed. And God can see beyond your current situation too, to a completely different time frame in your life when these financial difficulties are behind you.

Don't give up. There's life on the other side of your present circumstances, and it's a good life.

Father, I get so low sometimes when I look at the situations I face. I can get overwhelmed so easily. Thank You for the reminder that You see beyond my current status. There's life on the other side of it, so I won't give up. Thank You for that reminder. Amen.

Hope Doesn't Put Us to Shame

Therefore, since we have been justified by faith, we have peace with God through our Lord Jesus Christ. Through him we have also obtained access by faith into this grace in which we stand, and we rejoice in hope of the glory of God. Not only that, but we rejoice in our sufferings, knowing that suffering produces endurance, and endurance produces character, and character produces hope, and hope does not put us to shame, because God's love has been poured into our hearts through the Holy Spirit who has been given to us.

ROMANS 5:1–5

. . . .

She felt sure this job would last forever. Everything about it felt like a good fit. . .until it didn't. For a while, she tried to force the puzzle pieces to come together, convinced that time would solve the problem. She gave more of herself, pressed harder, worked smarter. That didn't solve the problem. After a while she could deny it no longer: she simply couldn't stay.

When the opportunity presented itself, she took flight—away from the problems, the turmoil, the emotional struggles—and toward a new job, a new life. In that new place, everything that had turned topsy-turvy felt right again. She managed to start over, this time without the added stresses she'd battled at the last place.

There's nothing easy about transitioning out of one job and

into another, though people are forced to do it all the time. Sometimes you're left with a damaged reputation, gossipers, and false accusations. But if you're in a position that seems unbearable to you, perhaps it's time to look elsewhere. And remember, God already sees into the future. He knows where you're going to land. He has promised in His Word that He won't leave you or forsake you. In fact, His Spirit will guide you to the very place you need to go, so you can trust Him completely.

This experience will build you into a stronger person. It will produce endurance, character, and all of the things listed in the scripture above. You're going to make it, and you'll be strong on the flip side, no doubt about it.

Father, I know You're building character in me. I won't despise the work You're doing, even when my circumstances are tough. I'll trust that You have my best interests at heart and that You're moving on my behalf even now. Amen.

Be Watchful

Stay alert! Watch out for your great enemy,
the devil. He prowls around like a roaring lion,
looking for someone to devour.

1 PETER 5:8 NLT

. . . .

We will never know for sure what prompted Esau to sell his birthright to his twin brother, Jacob, for a bowl of lentil stew, but we do know that Jacob was savvy. In one swift move, he shifted from second-born to first, from the overlooked child to bearer of the birthright, from spiritual lesser to spiritual greater. Talk about a shift in positioning! And all because he happened upon his twin brother at a vulnerable time and knew just what to say and do.

One has to wonder if, in the wee hours of the night, Esau regretted his decision, or if Jacob was ever filled with shame or remorse for striking such a bargain. Perhaps their parents, Isaac and Rebekah, tried to reason with them after the fact, to explain that such a thing just wasn't done.

Regardless, it *was* done, and Esau paid a hefty price. He lost his placement, his standing, his father's blessing. And Jacob maneuvered into a place he was never born to fill, that of inheritor. He was a sneaky one, that Jacob.

Of course, the wrangling between these two took place even before they were born. While they were still in their mother's womb they wrestled with each other. This was just a foreshadowing of things to come.

If you're not careful, the enemy of your soul can sneak in with a convincing speech, offering you the deal of a lifetime. Be careful! He's a trickster, intent on destroying you. Sure, his words are slick, but so is his motive. You won't just lose your birthright; he's out to take your very life. So keep your eyes wide open. Be on the lookout. He's prowling even now, but you're smarter than he is. And remember, there's power in the name of Jesus. The minute the enemy rears his ugly head, just shout that name. . .and watch him flee.

*Father, my eyes are wide open. I won't fall into any traps.
I won't let the enemy pull one over on me, no matter how slick
or polished his words might be. I'm right here, ready to take
my rightful place as Your child. I'll shout the name of Your
Son, Jesus—my Rock and my Redeemer! Amen.*

Forgetting What Lies Behind

Brothers, I do not consider that I have made it my own.
But one thing I do: forgetting what lies behind and straining
forward to what lies ahead, I press on toward the goal for
the prize of the upward call of God in Christ Jesus.
PHILIPPIANS 3:13–14

. . . .

Some people are more forgetful than others. They struggle to remember important dates—birthdays, anniversaries, business luncheons, and so on. They're embarrassed when a good friend or loved one has a birthday because—gasp!—they forgot. Again. Their forgetfulness isn't due to lack of caring. On the contrary, they care very much. They just can't seem to keep up with things like that.

Still others are distracted and forget to do simple things, like take their daily meds or pay the electric bill. Some can't seem to remember to keep up with the laundry or dishes. In this crazy, fast-paced world, there's a lot to forget!

Then there are folks who never forget a thing. They're always on top of the details of life. Bills are paid in advance. The clean dishes are always taken out of the dishwasher in a timely fashion. Laundry doesn't pile up. The car stays clean. They remember every birthday, every anniversary. They'd never forget a special occasion or an event at work. These folks really have their act together.

Where do you fall on this spectrum? Are you forgetful? Mindful? Fastidious? On top of things? Do you find yourself overlooking events or looking forward to them with great expectation?

No matter where you land on the "remembering" scale, there's one thing the Lord hopes you'll forget: the past. When you're hyper-focused on what happened yesterday, you carry the burden and unnecessary shame of yesterday. Talk about a time and energy waster! It's time to forget. . .on purpose.

Don't dredge up those old memories of the embarrassing or shameful things you did when you were younger. They're behind you now. They have no power over you. Point yourself in the direction of the calling of Christ on your life. He has a wonderful future for you if you can just stay focused on Him. Press on toward the goal. You'll be delighted at where God is taking you.

Father, I won't look back. I'll remember to forget. I'll press toward the goal that's right in front of me, Lord. I can't wait to see where the road will take me, now that I'm finally letting go of the past for good. Amen.

Alive in the Spirit

For Christ also suffered once for sins, the righteous for
the unrighteous, to bring you to God. He was put to
death in the body but made alive in the Spirit.
1 PETER 3:18 NIV

Have you ever pondered that phrase "death in the body"? It's one thing to die a natural death. We'll all face that at some point. But to deliberately put to death our carnal, fleshly desires? That's something the Bible commands us to do, hard as it might be. And there are plenty of areas in our lives that need to be put to death.

If we refuse to deal with desires that tug us away from God, then we'll suffer consequences that could go on for a lifetime. Every addict wishes they had buried their desires early on to avoid the chaos that ensued as a result of their choices. Every parent who ever lashed out at a child wishes they could take those words back and speak words of life instead.

So what "carnal desires" are you struggling with today? Overeating? Drinking? Crankiness? Lying? It's time to make a conscious decision to put those things to death. Picture yourself holding a funeral for your ungodly desires. Bury them deep into the ground, never to be seen or heard from again.

Here's the good news. God has made us alive in His Spirit. The Holy Spirit resides inside of us, giving us the power, the desire, and the wherewithal to do the right thing. Without the help of the Spirit, we lack the oomph. But being infused from the inside out, we have supernatural power.

Are you alive in the Spirit? Have you accepted Christ as Savior and received the gift of the Holy Spirit? Have you said goodbye to yesterday and hello to eternity? If not, today would be the perfect day to begin your spiritual journey. Christ died to bring us to God. His greatest desire is that you would be made alive in Him.

I'm so glad to be fully alive in Your Spirit, Lord! Gone are the days of shaming and blaming. I've put to death those desires that separated me from You. I'm Yours now, infused with power from on high and ready to do great things for Your kingdom. Amen.

He Bore It All

Surely he has borne our griefs and carried our sorrows;
yet we esteemed him stricken, smitten by God, and afflicted.
Isaiah 53:4

. . . .

She never meant for it to happen. Jeannie was a normal child with typical wishes and dreams. Sure, she loved to pacify herself with food, especially when kids at school made fun of her crooked teeth and curly hair, but so what? Didn't all kids love sweets? Nibbling on cookies and cupcakes didn't make her different, did it?

As she transitioned into her teen years, Jeannie turned more and more to food to squelch her woes. No date for the prom? Rocky road ice cream would make everything seem better. No invitation to the party? Pizza would solve that problem. Left out of the group that used to include her in elementary school? She'd show them—by binge-watching movies and downing more snacks.

More and more she found herself eating alone and consuming more than she should have. Sometimes she made special trips to the store to purchase sweets then ate them in the car and threw away the wrappers.

By the time Jeannie married and had children, she was fighting weight issues and psychological problems. She found it difficult to respond to marital problems, but cooking was a favorite pastime.

Nibbling as she cooked was a habit, one she didn't see as a problem. Until it began to affect her health. Type 2 diabetes reared its head, along with gastric problems and high blood pressure. The doctor shared his concerns, but she wasn't sure how to fix things at this point. How could she turn this train around, now that it was barreling down the track?

Perhaps you read Jeannie's story and feel a sense of connection to her. You've used food to pacify yourself, to make yourself feel better about the hard situations you've faced. "It's not like I'm drinking alcohol or taking drugs," you assure yourself. Still, in the quiet hours, as you finish off that pint of ice cream or that bag of chocolates, you wonder if you could give up this habit. What would happen if you had to?

This problem you're facing isn't bigger than the God who loves you. He has already carried your sorrows and struggles to the cross, after all. It's not too late to ask for His help and to get a handle on things. Together, you can work on a plan to set things right.

Father, I confess I often comfort myself with food. I need to be more conscious of this tendency. Will You help me figure out a way to get control of my appetite, Lord? I want to begin again. With Your help, I can. Amen.

Confidence When He Appears

And now, little children, abide in him, so that when
he appears we may have confidence and not
shrink from him in shame at his coming.
1 JOHN 2:28

. . . .

Have you ever wondered how or why God chose Moses to deliver His people out of Egypt? Why this man?

Maybe you recall Moses' unusual story. He grew up in the Egyptian palace as the adopted son of royalty. In spite of his upbringing, he never got over the horror of watching his own people, the Hebrews, suffer at the hands of Egyptian rulers. One day, as Moses looked on, one of the Hebrew slaves, a forced laborer, was beaten by an Egyptian taskmaster. The sight was more than Moses could take. He waited until no one was around, then beat the Egyptian to death. Afterward, he hid the man's body in the sand.

Whoa. This is not the Moses we're accustomed to reading about in Sunday school—the one who led his people through the Red Sea, the one who climbed the mountain and came down with the Ten Commandments, the one who met with God in the holy of holies. This is a different fellow altogether.

Meet Moses the rash one. Moses the murderer. Moses, the one who snapped in defense of his Hebrew brother. This was the man God chose to deliver His people?

Here's the truth: God can use anyone, even folks who've messed up. If you read the Bible from cover to cover, you'll see this pattern repeated over and over again. He used flawed people to accomplish great things, even people who carried shame and guilt.

God can use you too. You're not Moses. You won't deliver your people, at least not physically. But maybe He will use you to deliver your family from darkness into God's marvelous light. Perhaps He'll use you to turn situations around at your workplace. Maybe the Lord will use you to intervene in the life of a child in need. There are countless ways you can—and will—be used as a deliverer.

Brace yourself! Deliverance is ahead!

Father, I long to be used by You, as Moses was used to deliver his people. There are so many people in my world who are in turmoil, in need of deliverance. I want to play a role, Lord. Show me how, I pray. Amen.

Worthy to Suffer Dishonor

The apostles left the high council rejoicing that God had counted them worthy to suffer disgrace for the name of Jesus.
ACTS 5:41 NLT

From the time of the disciples until now, believers have suffered persecution at the hands of those who oppose their message. Over the years, many have been martyred for their faith, simply because they refused to conform to the secular (or even religious) teachings of their day. Some of our current struggles pale in comparison, but rumblings against the Christian faith are still out there, some subtle, others like an ever-growing drumbeat, intent on wiping out the message of Christ altogether.

Gordon-Conwell's Center for the Study of Global Christianity estimates that nearly a million Christians were martyred over the past decade. That's a shocking and staggering number. More than three hundred believers die every month for their faith. Think of the number of people in your circle of friends. Can you even imagine losing one as a result of persecution? It's unfathomable, and yet it happens every day.

We're taught in scripture not to be ashamed of our faith. It is life-giving, after all. But it's not always easy to speak the name of Jesus publicly. In fact, it's getting harder every day, even in places where the Gospel was once welcomed with open arms.

There are those who would do their best to cause shame or point fingers of blame, saying believers must conform their thinking to what the world says.

What do you say about that? Is it getting harder for you to take a stand for what you believe? As you study this verse, as you recognize that the apostles rejoiced that God counted them worthy to suffer dishonor for the name of Jesus, how does their boldness impact you? Are you of the same mind-set, or are you more tempted to keep your mouth shut and not tell others about your faith? It's time for the modern church to have a real discussion about what it means to stand firm in the faith, despite opposition. And it's time to recommit ourselves to the mind-set of the apostles. It really is an honor to suffer disgrace for the sake of the Gospel.

There's much to think about as the world moves farther away from the One who created it. What can you do to take a stand?

Lord, I want to be found faithful during these last days. If that means I have to suffer dishonor for Your name, then so be it. I would rather stay true to my faith than to give in to the temptation to stop sharing my faith. Keep me strong, I pray. Amen.

A Beautiful Covering

And her husband Joseph, being a just man and unwilling to put her to shame, resolved to divorce her quietly.

MATTHEW 1:19

. . . .

Have you ever paused to really think through the story of Mary and Joseph? Both were faced with an unimaginable task—to convince people that they had maintained their purity while also sharing the news that a baby was on the way.

Can you even imagine what the gossips in the village had to say when the news broke? If this happened in the twenty-first century, social media would be buzzing. Talking heads would argue counterpoints. The medical community would sign in with their take on things. Politicians would argue about whether or not the baby deserved to live. And Christians would be split down the middle, as they so often are.

Back in Mary and Joseph's day, things weren't much different, though it surely took longer for the gossips to spread their stories. The scuttlebutt must've been crazy. Poor Mary had enough to worry about. She was carrying the Savior of the world, after all. And Joseph! Can you even imagine what must have gone through his mind the moment he had the "Guess what—we're having a baby!" conversation with his intended?

Joseph, filled with shame over their situation, made up his

mind to put Mary away quietly. He didn't want to make a public spectacle out of her, after all. Still, he wanted to opt out of their upcoming marriage agreement because the current situation was just too hard to bear.

Then God interrupted his plan and sent an angel to encourage Joseph in his despair. He walked away from that angelic encounter a changed man. From that point on, he was in. . .100 percent. He went on to accept the role of father to the young Messiah and husband to Mary. He raised his son to be a carpenter, a good man.

Aren't you glad Joseph took the time to get past what he was feeling and listen to God's thoughts on his situation? Maybe it's time for you to do the same. Put your own feelings aside—even if you're struggling with shock or despair—and listen for the Lord's opinion on what you're going through. His perspective is the one that matters most.

Father, I want Your perspective. I don't want to base my decisions on feelings. I'll wait until I hear from You, Lord. Then I'll move accordingly. Amen.

Perfected in Love

There is no fear in love. But perfect love drives out fear,
because fear has to do with punishment. The one
who fears is not made perfect in love.
1 John 4:18 NIV

- -

The idea of hosting a small group at your house sounds wonderful, until you think about the condition your house is in. You're ashamed of how things look. With so much on your plate, you've hardly had time to keep up with things. The kitchen faucet is leaking again. The dog has ruined a section of the carpet in your hallway. Laundry is piled up on the sofa, and the kids have left their craft projects all over the kitchen table. The baseboards are dingy, the countertops are chipped, and the furniture is woefully outdated. Ordinarily these things don't bother you, not much, anyway. But when you visit the homes of the other ladies from church, you see how much effort has been put into making those homes look perfect. And it seems too unattainable for you.

Try as you may, you can't seem to keep your house looking the way you want. It's a never-ending struggle, one you don't appear to be winning. You've tried to tackle things one room at a time, one project at a time, but your work schedule and the kids' after-school activities are keeping you away from the house more than in it. Sure, the broken light fixture in the hall bugs you, but not enough to purchase a new one, climb a ladder, and put it up.

So what's a gal to do. . .continue to hide in her mess?

The answer to that question is a resounding "No!" God has given you a home, and it's time to start sharing it. Do what you can to prepare, but stop saying no to having friends over because you're ashamed of your house. They won't care. Better still, if you're really fretting over the condition of things, invite a friend over to help you organize or paint or replace that broken light fixture. You'll have designated time together and get something accomplished at the same time.

God has blessed you with your home, and it's time to share the blessing. No more excuses!

Father, it's hard to get past the embarrassment when I look at some of the rooms in my home. Show me how to tackle the various projects, but also give me courage to get past my shame so that I can feel comfortable with people in my home. Amen.

Resting in His Steadfast Love

Give thanks to the LORD, for he is good; his love endures forever. Let Israel say: "His love endures forever." Let the house of Aaron say: "His love endures forever." Let those who fear the LORD say: "His love endures forever." When hard pressed, I cried to the LORD; he brought me into a spacious place. The LORD is with me; I will not be afraid. What can mere mortals do to me? The LORD is with me; he is my helper. I look in triumph on my enemies.

PSALM 118:1–7 NIV

· ·

"I'm not talented." "I'm not pretty." "I'm not smart." How many times have you used words like these? "I can't sing." "I can't hold down a job." "I'll never have a husband." On and on the list goes. You have the dialogue memorized; you've spoken the lines so often.

But why? Why do you beat yourself up?

It's time to figure out whose lens you are viewing yourself through. Is it God's lens, or perhaps the lens of someone who spoke harsh, judgmental words over you years ago? If you're hanging on to someone else's proclamation of who or what you are, it's time to let go of that assessment and move on.

When you have an incorrect view of yourself, it affects everything.

Imagine you made an appointment to see an eye specialist.

She analyzed your vision and decided you needed glasses. You picked out a really cute pair. They looked just right with your face shape. When you went to pick them up, the prescribed glasses made your vision ten times worse, not better. But you continued to wear them, hoping you would acclimate and that your vision would ultimately improve. Only, it never did.

That's what it's like when you examine yourself through the wrong lens. Things never get better. They only get worse. It's time to replace the lens. Do away with those negative words that were spoken over you. Get in the Word and see what God says about you. You can rest in His love and His encouragement. He won't cut you down. In fact, He's all about lifting you up.

Grab those new glasses and see what He sees. He thinks you're pretty amazing, after all.

Father, I'll trade in my old glasses for new. I'll begin to see myself differently. My lenses are a terrible fit, Lord. I need Your point of view, Your perspective. With You, I'll have 20/20 vision, Father. I'm so grateful for this newfound clarity. Amen.

Walk in Wisdom

Whoever trusts in his own mind is a fool,
but he who walks in wisdom will be delivered.
PROVERBS 28:26

. . . .

Judas Iscariot. Just the mention of his name brings a shiver to the spine. Betrayer. Knife-in-the-back, would-be friend. He represents all that we, as Christians, try not to be. To turn our backs on Jesus, as he did, would be unthinkable.

Before he was Judas the betrayer, though, he was Judas the apostle. Judas, the man chosen by Jesus to walk alongside Him, to watch Jesus pray for the sick, to witness miracles, to minister to the needy. He was a brother, a companion, a fellow traveler, a friend, one who never had any intention of turning his back on the One he loved. He prayed for the sick, loved his friends, and was perfectly content to spend time at the feet of Jesus, learning from his Master.

He was, in short, just like the rest of the disciples. Just like us. And then, in a moment that would change the course of history, this ordinary man made a terrible decision to betray his best friend. He turned his back on the One he loved. . .for thirty pieces of silver. He sold Him out.

Maybe you've been betrayed by a Judas, a person you had trusted as a true friend. You've experienced the twisting of the knife in your back as someone you once loved caught you off guard. This betrayal stung. It cut deep and made you question every other relationship, as you wondered who would betray you next.

The truth is we all have a Judas story, whether we're the recipient of betrayal or the one with the coins in our hands. People are fickle. They turn on a dime. They're loyal one minute, then turn their backs on you the next. That's why we need the wisdom of the Lord to help us navigate life's relationships.

There's really only one friend you can count on never to betray you. His name is Jesus. He has experienced betrayal at the hands of humankind, but He will never turn His back on you, no matter what.

Father, sometimes I don't even know if I can trust myself. I care deeply about a friend, then my emotions shift and I don't seem to care at all. I'm as fickle as anyone else. I need Your wisdom, Lord, to navigate the precious friendships You've given me. Help me, I pray. Amen.

Step Away from the Fire

And what was the result? You are now ashamed of the things you used to do, things that end in eternal doom.
Romans 6:21 NLT

. . . .

Ginny just kept going back to those same old patterns. She would walk in freedom for a season, completely released from the pain and heartache of the past. Then something would happen to trigger an emotional knee-jerk reaction, and off she would go. . .back to her old way of living. Oh, she never did it deliberately. In fact, she tried to fight it. And she suffered shame and regret every single time. But she just couldn't seem to stop repeating the learned behaviors and patterns. They felt comfortable. Familiar.

Maybe you can relate to Ginny. There are areas of your life that you'd like to keep in the past. In fact, you would prefer that no one else found out about the person you used to be. Alcohol abuse. Temper tantrums. Cheating. Lying. Pornography. Overeating. Oh, so many things you'd like to bury away and forget about. But every now and again something happens to open old wounds. When that happens, you turn, once again, to that thing you swore you'd never do again. You reach for the bottle. You eat that Italian cream cake. Your temper flares and you lash out at people you love. You cheat on your spouse. You turn to gambling. And you're filled with instant regret, because those things were never meant to bring eternal satisfaction or joy.

Being set free from sin isn't a simple process. Sure, Jesus forgives instantly, but shaking off old patterns takes awhile. So don't beat yourself up. But do make yourself accountable to someone you trust—a fellow believer, a pastor, a counselor—someone who will help you walk through this season.

Remember, falling off the wagon doesn't mean you're a failure. You might've failed this time, but there are plenty of opportunities to get it right in the future. So make whatever restitution needs to be made then climb back up on that wagon and begin again.

Father, I get so angry with myself for falling off the wagon.
I don't mean to do it. Please forgive me for the damage
I've done. I need Your help starting again, Lord.
Please point me toward a friend who can help
hold me accountable, I pray. Amen.

Strong Confidence

Those who fear the LORD are secure;
he will be a refuge for their children.
PROVERBS 14:26 NLT

She often wonders if getting a real job might be for the best. This stay-at-home-mom gig is hard and doesn't come with a lot of accolades. Seems like she's always changing diapers, washing clothes, sweeping floors, wiping off high chairs, or cooking. It's an endless cycle, day in and day out, a routine that rarely changes. And no matter how hard she tries, she can't seem to keep her house as clean as she would like. There are just too many people underfoot to accomplish that.

Sometimes she ponders her options. Maybe it's time to get a job. Working moms seem to have it easier. They can escape to their workplace during the day and come home to kiddos after school is out. They can have lunch with a friend or talk about something other than the latest animated show for toddlers.

Still, her heart is torn. Right now, the little ones need her. And she wants to be there for them. Her husband agrees. There might be time for a job later, but for now her place is here, at home. And she's doing her best to settle in for the long haul.

So why does she feel guilty? Is it the looks she receives from other moms who work outside the home? Is it the fact that her little family gets by on less money than others? Is it because some people think she's lazy or unwilling to get a real job? She feels bad enough that her husband has to work so hard to cover the mortgage and the car payment. Shouldn't she be helping with all of that instead of picking up cereal crumbs from the kitchen floor?

Here's the truth, Mama: Staying home with your children is nothing to be ashamed of. Being a mom is one of the highest callings in the world, and if you're blessed to be able to stay home with your children during those formative years, why not? Enjoy them while you can. These days are short, after all. Don't let anyone shame you into thinking you need to get a "real" job. The job you have right now is plenty real enough.

I'm going to try not to focus too much on what other people think about my parenting decisions, Lord. It's no one else's business, anyway. I'll keep following Your lead, doing what You've called me to do. Amen.

Never Condemned

Affliction will slay the wicked, and those who hate the righteous will be condemned. The LORD redeems the life of his servants; none of those who take refuge in him will be condemned.

PSALM 34:21–22

. . . .

Seventy-eight candles lit the birthday cake, giving off a blaze so bright the man had to squint. Was he really expected to blow them all out with one breath? It seemed impossible, and yet the roomful of guests urged him on with claps and cheers. Nearly thirty seconds later, with the help of a grandchild or two, he managed to get the job done. The crowd sang a rousing chorus of "Happy Birthday," and he settled back in his chair, ready for a piece of cake.

As he surveyed the room, the man couldn't help but be overcome with emotions. He didn't deserve this life—the wife of fifty-two years, the three children, the eight grands. He didn't deserve the birthday cake, the song, the pats on the back, the love. He didn't deserve any of it, and yet the Lord had seen fit to give it all to him, a priceless gift in spite of his mistakes. His regrets.

All of those years he'd wasted, his head in a bottle. All of those memories, lost and unaccounted for. All of those opportunities, wasted. What he wouldn't give to have them all back again. To toss those bottles of alcohol into the trash can. To kiss his wife and tell her she was worth every bit of his time. To tell his children how sorry he was for missing ballet recitals and basketball games. To read more stories to his grandchildren. He would gladly ask for a redo, if only life worked like that.

Maybe you sense this man's struggle. Perhaps you've lost a few years as well. Here's the good news: God is a redeemer, not just of people, but of time. Ask Him to redeem the years you have left so that you can leave a legacy for those you love, one that will bring a smile to their faces long after you're gone.

I know we all have regrets, Lord. I have more than a few. But I refuse to focus on those. Right now I want to ask You to help with the years I have left on this planet. You're the Great Redeemer, Lord. Please redeem the time, I pray. Amen.

Caught in the Act

For all have sinned and fall short of the glory of God.
ROMANS 3:23 NIV

. . . .

Caught in the very act of adultery. Can you even imagine what the woman must have been thinking and feeling as she was dragged from the bedroom of the man she was sleeping with? Her accusers flung her onto the ground at the feet of a man she didn't even recognize. Jesus, they called Him. She didn't know this man, but the others seemed to think He was some sort of religious leader. No doubt He would be the first to throw a stone.

His followers seemed disgusted by her, but Jesus glanced down with such tenderness in His expression, it caught her off guard. She could not fathom such a reaction. Ten thousand words tried to escape her lips at once, but she could not speak. She braced herself for the stoning that she knew would come. Instead, she listened, stunned, as the man spoke to the others: "Let him who is without sin among you be the first to throw a stone at her" (John 8:7).

Her heart thumped madly as she tried to make sense of the phrase. Surely one of them would reach for a stone and hurl it her way. She flinched in preparation. Would this be her last day of life? Would they finish what they started and take her very life?

One by one, her accusers left. Alone with Jesus and His

followers, she stared up into His compassionate eyes. Shame washed over her, but He did not accuse. Instead, He looked at her with great tenderness and said, "Woman, where are your accusers?"

She looked around, relieved to see they had all disappeared, leaving her alone with this remarkable man, the One with love radiating from every pore. How could He show such love, such grace? What could she ever do to repay Him?

Perhaps you can relate to this woman. You've been caught in the very act of sin more than once. Instead of pointing fingers, the Lord pulled you close and reminded you that you're not alone. All have sinned and fallen short of His glory. Though sin separates humankind from God, the blood of Jesus serves as the great mediator, closing the gap. Aren't you grateful for a Savior who makes all things new?

Lord, I can't thank You enough. You don't stand as my accuser. You stand as my Rescuer. You've pulled me up from the pit of humiliation and despair and set my feet on a rock. I'm so grateful, Father. Amen.

Forgotten

"Fear not, for you will not be ashamed; be not confounded, for you will not be disgraced; for you will forget the shame of your youth, and the reproach of your widowhood you will remember no more."

ISAIAH 54:4

. . . .

No one plans to be ill. In fact, most people don't think long-term chronic illness will ever happen to them. But many—men, women, and children—suffer with ongoing issues like autoimmune diseases, including arthritis, fibromyalgia, and so on. Others are born with issues that require lifelong care.

Perhaps you are one of those who struggles with chronic illness or pain. These battles can be lengthy, expensive, and frustrating. Unkind acquaintances, coworkers, and even loved ones who don't see visible symptoms can be unnecessarily cruel as they question how you're feeling. Maybe their words aren't meant to be accusing, but they sure sound that way. And you don't have easy answers. Oh, how you'd love to say, "I'm feeling great, thanks for asking!" But you can't.

So what's a weary sufferer to do? Battling pain is one thing, but tacking on shame is another, altogether. Just getting through the very real physical issues you're facing is exhausting enough. God never intended for you to bear the shame associated with chronic illness on top of what you're already going through.

First, start by forgiving those who don't understand. They've never walked a mile in your shoes. They truly don't get it. But it's not your place to convince them. Best to put their opinions out of your mind. Next, give yourself some grace. Give your body adequate time to heal. Don't push yourself so hard. Who cares if you need more recovery time after big events? So what if the laundry isn't done right away? You need to take care of you. Finally, don't be ashamed of what you're dealing with. You didn't cause this, and you're doing the best you can to adapt to your circumstances. Just stick close to the Lord and let Him show you how to tackle each day as it comes.

Father, I've been in a lot of pain over the years, and sometimes it causes me to lash out at others. Today I choose to forgive those who've criticized or made fun of me. I know they don't understand, Lord. Help me focus on You, not them. And heal me, I pray. I won't give up, Lord. Amen.

When I Consider. . .

When I consider your heavens, the work of your fingers,
the moon and the stars, which you have set in place,
what is mankind that you are mindful of them,
human beings that you care for them?
Psalm 8:3–4 niv

Galaxies spin as if they've been called upon to perform a magnificent ballet before their Maker. Sun, moon, and stars twinkle, a reflection of the light of their Master Designer. They hang in space, beautifully placed, just as He intended. The whole of creation stands as a testament to the living God, the Creator of all. What an amazing designer He is! Isn't it remarkable to know that He created it all with us in mind?

With so many things to look after, you might wonder how the Lord manages to know every detail about you. You are, after all, microscopic in comparison. Shouldn't He be looking after Saturn or Mars? Shouldn't He be concerned about the rising of the sun or the tug of the tide? Shouldn't He keep His gaze on countries in great turmoil? Is He really going to take precious time to spend with you in the midst of all of that?

The truth is you are even more important to God than any planet, any wonder of nature. You're His bright star, and He cherishes you above all. He's mindful of every little thing about you—the way you laugh, that splattering of freckles on your nose, your crooked smile. He's watching over you twenty-four hours a day, seven days a week. He's not an absentminded parent; instead, He's ever watchful, making sure you have all you need to get through this life.

So consider the heavens. But while you're considering them, remember that you're the center of your heavenly Father's galaxy. He has His eyes firmly fixed on you and wants you to know that you are deeply loved.

We serve an amazing, miraculous God. He could be doing anything (and everything) right now, but He has chosen to focus on you, His child. Now that's a miracle worth celebrating!

It boggles my mind that You take the time to be with me when there are ten billion other things You could be doing right now. (You're a great multitasker, by the way!) When I consider Your great creation, I stand in awe that You would take the time to care for me. Oh, how grateful I am! Thank You, Father. Amen.

Victorious Power

Now this I know: The LORD gives victory to his anointed. He answers him from his heavenly sanctuary with the victorious power of his right hand.

PSALM 20:6 NIV

. . . .

Sometimes we simply forget how powerful God is. We get so wrapped up in thinking that everything depends on us that we miss the obvious—everything is in God's hands. Remember, this is the same God who spoke the earth into existence. With the tip of a finger, He carved mountains. With a breath, He formed winds. With the palm of His hand He made ocean waves rise and fall. With the flick of a finger He sent millions of stars twirling out into space to light the night sky. He put moons, suns, and planets in place. And He sustains everything without asking our permission or seeking our input.

This is no wimpy Creator we're talking about. He can populate the earth with vegetation in an instant and take it all away with forty days of floodwaters. He can send snow in the winter and can color the leaves in the fall. He can speak into situations and change them for all eternity.

Putting God in His rightful place (as Author, Creator, and King) helps us trust Him with the things we're going through. It also helps us realize that we control nothing. God is the One who determines what will happen. He knows the whys and wherefores. We don't need to know. We just need to trust.

But He doesn't leave us powerless. We have authority in the name of Jesus. Something amazing happens in the heavenlies when we speak that amazing name. Demons have to flee, mountains have to bow, all of creation has to respond to that one word: *Jesus*.

When was the last time you used the name of Jesus as your defense? Don't let life beat you down. You don't have to cave when hard times come. Stand tall and speak the name of Jesus, then watch as the heavens open and miracles happen.

Jesus, how I love to speak Your name! I'm so grateful for the power it brings. I don't have to depend on myself. I don't have to be tied to the woes of this life or the shameful things I've done in the past. I'm completely free, thanks to Your wonder-working power. Amen.

Swallowed by the Sea

Once again you will have compassion on us. You will trample our sins under your feet and throw them into the depths of the ocean!

MICAH 7:19 NLT

Picture a young woman in a small life raft. She's adrift at sea, wondering if she will ever make it safely back to shore. She's carrying a large weight, which is causing the raft to sink. The weight serves no purpose. She could be rid of it at any time, but she doesn't know how to let go. In fact, she seems to find her identity in the weight, so she clings even tighter to it than before.

Every minute counts as she tries to figure out how to stay afloat. Before long, the waves are crashing over the edges of the raft, threatening to take it down. Something needs to be done, and quickly.

In desperation, she hurls the weight overboard. It sinks to the bottom of the sea. The raft pops up above the waves, relieved of its burden. In that moment, the woman sees her first glimpses of hope. She will not drown. She's now free to paddle herself to shore, unencumbered.

Maybe you can relate to this woman. You've often felt adrift and riddled with fear. The weights of yesterday have held you captive and threatened to pull you under. Instead of tossing the weights, you held to them tighter than ever. You found your identity in the very thing that was dragging you down.

God wants you to know that He stands ready to hurl the shame of your yesterdays overboard. If you'll let Him release it to the bottom of the sea, you can move forward freely, much like the woman in this story.

What weights are you holding today? Are they slowing things down or threatening to drown you? Make a conscious decision to let go of them right now so that you can live your life completely unencumbered.

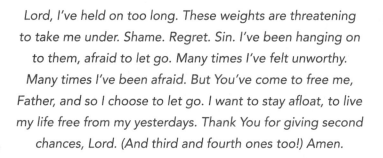

Lord, I've held on too long. These weights are threatening to take me under. Shame. Regret. Sin. I've been hanging on to them, afraid to let go. Many times I've felt unworthy. Many times I've been afraid. But You've come to free me, Father, and so I choose to let go. I want to stay afloat, to live my life free from my yesterdays. Thank You for giving second chances, Lord. (And third and fourth ones too!) Amen.

I Have Hoped in Your Word

May those who fear you rejoice when they see me,
for I have put my hope in your word.
PSALM 119:74 NIV

. . . .

He felt the aloneness most whenever he went to church. Ever since his wife passed away, things just weren't the same. So many of the couples around him still carried on in their usual way, but his beautiful bride wasn't here to complete him anymore. He was flying solo. Even sitting in his usual pew felt strange. She had always filled the spot next to him, after all.

His friends didn't do it on purpose, but he felt left out at times. Their usual couples' events just weren't the same without his wife, so he found himself staying home more and more these days. No one deliberately ostracized him or made him feel unwelcome, but the whole social scene at church just felt. . .uncomfortable. He was embarrassed and sad to walk through that door without his wife at his side. So he opted out. And as time went by, he found himself deeper and deeper in loneliness. Because he hadn't just lost *her*. . .he'd lost *them*.

If you've lost a loved one, you know the sting of this story. Going from two to one is extremely difficult, whether you've lost a spouse who passed away or gone through a divorce. Many church events (and life events) are couples-centered. Now you're not a couple. It's just you. And you don't know where you fit in anymore.

Take heart! Your situation might have changed, but God has not. He wants you to maintain relationships, even if it's hard. And He has new relationships on the horizon for you as well. There are other newly single folks out there feeling just like you. Maybe it's time to attend a support group or start a Bible study for singles just like you.

There's reason to hope, even after losing a mate. God will walk with you every step of the way. Keep your trust in Him and don't give up.

Father, sometimes I feel so lost and alone. It's hard not to be jealous of those who still have their mate. But I feel Your presence keenly. I know You're with me, and that brings me great comfort. I won't let my feelings control my future, Lord. I'll keep moving forward. Amen.

Upright

Those nations will fall down and collapse,
but we will rise up and stand firm.
PSALM 20:8 NLT

. . . .

If you're a *Pride and Prejudice* fan, you know the humiliation Lizzy Bennet suffered at the hands of her foolish younger sisters and her over-the-top, money-hungry mama. On more than one occasion she found herself cringing or wanting to run out the door. But where would she go?

Lizzy found it difficult to move in society because her family members embarrassed her at every turn. Who would want to marry a girl who came from such a crazy family, after all? She was destined to remain a spinster forever if something didn't change, and right now nothing seemed to be changing.

In reality, Lizzy was embarrassed and ashamed of her family's actions, but she couldn't voice those feelings aloud. It wasn't proper in those days for a single young woman to contradict her mother or meddle in the affairs of her sisters. Neither could she control them. Still, Lizzy secretly felt cheated because she knew her loved ones' antics would have far-reaching consequences that would affect her personally.

Maybe you can relate to Lizzy Bennet. Maybe you see your family (or people in your close inner circle) as odd ducks. They don't know how to behave in public. They're embarrassing. They're always saying or doing inappropriate things.

We all have those relatives, don't we? But what can we do about it?

It's important to be yourself and to set yourself apart from those who behave foolishly. You can't control what those around you are doing, but you can control yourself. Let others see, by comparison, that you're stable, solid, and set apart for God's work. This doesn't mean you have to ostracize your family members, but it might mean taking more time apart from them so you don't get caught up in the family drama.

This is a tricky one, isn't it? You love your family, but you love God even more. Pray fervently for those in turmoil and don't give up. But do what you can to protect yourself from the chaos while you're at it.

Father, I love my family and close friends, but sometimes they're a little crazy. The drama is over the top. Please show me how to function as a family member without getting drawn into the chaos. I want to represent You, Lord—with clean hands and a pure heart. Amen.

Sing for Joy

But let all who take refuge in you be glad; let them ever sing for joy. Spread your protection over them, that those who love your name may rejoice in you.

PSALM 5:11 NIV

. . . .

Refuge. Don't you love that word? Picture a wounded animal, barely hanging on to life. He's been attacked, almost killed, by a more vicious predator. He makes his way to a cave, thinking the end is near. There, in that quiet, peaceful place, he sleeps. . .and healing comes. The cave is his refuge, a place of safety from the outside world. It provides the perfect location for healing. It's sheltered. It's dark. The temperature is just right. More than anything, it's a place free from other wildlife. It's his own special healing place.

God is your refuge. He's your hiding place, your shelter from the storms of life. According to this scripture, He spreads His protection over you. Isn't that a lovely image? He takes a blanket and strategically places it over you when you're hurting.

No matter how badly you've been wounded, what shame you've faced, what poor decisions you've made, you can run to Him and find rest and peace. There, under the shadow of His wings, all of the broken places inside of you—the hurts, the negative words spoken over you, the heartache, the physical pain—can subside. You can think more clearly, pray with greater effective-ness, and begin to hope again. In fact, this verse even says that you can sing for joy! (When was the last time you spontaneously burst into song?)

When you hide yourself away in God's holy presence, He can restore your joy. The song, once dead forever, springs to life again. Before long, the pain is a distant memory. All that remains is the hopefulness of today and a bright future tomorrow.

What's holding you back? Head to your hiding place with the Savior right now.

Jesus, thank You for being my hiding place, my refuge! I'm so grateful to have a place to run to when the world beats me up. I bring all of my shame, my pain, my inner turmoil. I run into Your arms and collapse at Your feet. I give it all to You, and You turn things around. How I praise You for the work You're doing in my life, the restoration that's coming. Thank You, Lord. Amen.

Brought to Completion

And I am sure of this, that he who began a good work in you will bring it to completion at the day of Jesus Christ.

PHILIPPIANS 1:6

. . . .

God spoke to Abram and told him that he would be the father of many nations. What a remarkable promise! Can you imagine how excited Abram must have been as he thought ahead to the generations to come? His legacy would be remarkable, his offspring blessed.

As the years ticked by, Abram surely began to question the Lord's words. After all, he and Sarai were getting older and there were no babies. After a while, he began to wonder if maybe he'd somehow misunderstood God's message.

Without a shred of hope to conceive her own child, Sarai concocted a plan. She convinced Abram to sleep with her servant, Hagar, in the hopes that a child would come of the union. Her plan worked and Ishmael was born, but he was not the child of promise God had in mind.

Whether they ever admitted it to each other or not, Sarai and Abram got ahead of God with this foolish plan of theirs. They wanted to do things their own way. But that is never a good idea, as you've likely learned in your own walk with God.

In the end, the Lord still honored His word. He did what He

said He would do. Sarai conceived in her ripe old age and gave birth to the promised one, Isaac. The rest of biblical history was affected by the Lord's fulfillment of this promise. Abram really did become the father of many nations.

When you think of Abram and Sarai's rash decision to produce a child with Hagar, what comes to mind? Have you ever been so determined, so intent to see something come about that you did something shameful to make it happen? Maybe you wanted so desperately to pass the test that you cheated. Or maybe you wanted the job so badly that you somehow nudged the other candidate out of the way.

God is not keen on these sorts of actions. He will bring things to completion in His time and His way. Until then, just keep hanging on.

Father, I'm embarrassed and ashamed of myself for the many times I've gotten ahead of You. Please forgive me and show me how to trust You. If You say You'll do it. . .You'll do it. I choose to put my trust in You, Lord. Amen.

The Lifter of My Head

But you, LORD, are a shield around me,
my glory, the One who lifts my head high.
PSALM 3:3 NIV

You're buried deep in the miry clay of financial woes. You feel completely stuck. You started out ankle-deep. Then the debt rose to your knees. Now it's waist-deep, and you can sense that the situation is only going to get worse before it gets better. You don't know what to do to turn things around. No matter how high you toss those bills into the air, they land faceup, in need of paying. And you don't have the funds to cover them all. You're ashamed of yourself for letting things get to this point, in part because your impulsive spending brought you here. But you want to start over, to clear your name and begin again. Other people have done it. Can't you?

It's not too late for God to turn your situation around. He sees your heart and is proud of you for wanting to make a fresh start. And remember, He's all about fresh starts. If you read the Bible from cover to cover, you'll see dozens of people who thought they were washed up. God gave every single one a chance to make things right. He's the lifter of your head, the One who gives you a new sense of purpose when you go through "How did I get here?" seasons like the one you're in right now.

God longs to see you set free, and He has a plan to get you there. Start by making yourself accountable—to Him and to a friend. Create a plan, then stick with it. This won't be easy. It took awhile to get into this mess, and it will take awhile to get out. But you can do it with His help. Sure, it might be embarrassing. You might have to say no to your usual lunch dates. Or you might not get that new dress for the business event. But in the end you'll be in much better shape, financially and psychologically.

Sometimes I feel like I've painted myself into a corner, Lord. I do something impulsive and then live to regret it later. I don't deserve Your grace when I mess up, but You offer it anyway. For that, I'm extremely grateful. Amen.

Full Assurance of Hope

And we desire each one of you to show the same earnestness to have the full assurance of hope until the end.
HEBREWS 6:11

. . . .

The woman sat at her father's hospital bedside, tears flowing. She prayed, as always, that God would heal her dad and relieve him of this terrible pain and sickness. She couldn't bear to see him suffering like this. He'd done nothing to deserve such pain. In fact, he'd lived an exemplary life, serving God and loving others. He deserved peace. He deserved healing.

Despite her prayers, however, he continued to decline. . .and nothing about the situation made sense to her.

When that inevitable moment came—when he crossed over from this life to the next—she was completely undone. If she'd prayed harder, longer, more faithfully, maybe he would still be here. If she'd kept a better eye on him leading up to his diagnosis, maybe he would have stood a better chance. If she had chosen a different doctor, a different hospital, maybe he would still be here with her.

So many would'ves, could'ves, should'ves.

You've likely been through a similar situation. Perhaps the enemy has tormented you with all of the things you should have done. You're haunted by the death of a loved one, or maybe you've taken on the blame for someone's life-changing accident. Perhaps you blame yourself because a child has turned to alcohol or drugs. Or maybe you hold yourself responsible for a loved one's rejection of God.

The truth is only the Lord knows the number of our days, and our lives are in His hands. He alone knows when the moment will come for us to pass over from life to eternal life with Him. Even if we had done all of those things we're now wishing we'd done, the outcome might have been the same.

We have to trust God, even in the darkest hours. And we have to let go of any misplaced shame related to a loved one's death, illness, or rejection of God. We're not the ones in control, after all. God is. . .and He has a plan far greater than can be seen with the human eye.

I've carried the weight of things that were beyond my control, Father. Thank You for easing my pain. . .and my heart and mind. I trust You, Lord. I trust You. Amen.

Innocence

*Adam and his wife were both naked, and they felt no shame.
Now the serpent was more crafty than any of the wild animals
the LORD God had made. He said to the woman, "Did God
really say, 'You must not eat from any tree in the garden'?"*

GENESIS 2:25–3:1 NIV

Isn't it fun to watch children at play? As toddlers, they have such an innocence about them. Their little hearts are so tender and sweet. Whether they're playing with the puppy or kissing that newborn baby brother on the cheek, little ones are adorable.

Until they're not.

As they grow, the "me, myself, and I" mentality kicks in. Somewhere around age two they learn the word *no* and use it often, usually in defiance of their parents. By the time they hit the teen years, chaos often ensues. There's only so much self-centeredness a parent can take, after all. And if you're dealing with more than one, watch out! They don't always get along.

Now think about Adam and Eve in the garden. In many ways, they were like babes, fresh from the womb. There was an innocence about them. Their hearts—toward God and each other—were tender and sweet. Then enter the serpent, that crafty devil. He shifted their focus from God. . .to self. In an unexpected twist to the story, they immediately recognized their nakedness and found fig leaves to cover themselves. Interesting, right?

See a correlation? We've been fighting the "me, myself, and I" issue ever since Adam and Eve first bit into that forbidden fruit. When we come into this world, we are born (as Adam and Eve were created) naked and unashamed. No newborn ever cries out, "Put some clothes on me! Quick!" They're oblivious. That's the beauty of innocence. But once sin enters the picture, we're ready to cover everything up. We don't want others to see what we've done. We hide away in shadows, unwilling to let the light shine on our attitudes and actions.

Today God wants you to step out of the shadows and return to a life of purity, one where all is laid bare before Him. He can restore you to the innocence of a child, if you ask Him.

Father, thank You for the reminder that You can restore my purity. I want to be vulnerable before You, an open book. Take my eyes off myself, I pray, and keep them focused solely on You. Amen.

Get Up

As Peter traveled about the country, he went to visit the Lord's people who lived in Lydda. There he found a man named Aeneas, who was paralyzed and had been bedridden for eight years. "Aeneas," Peter said to him, "Jesus Christ heals you. Get up and roll up your mat." Immediately Aeneas got up. All those who lived in Lydda and Sharon saw him and turned to the Lord.

ACTS 9:32–35 NIV

. . . .

Eight years. Eight long, hopeless years doing the same thing day in and day out. Aeneas knew no other life than the one he lived on his mat. Destitute, broken, without hope, he simply tried to make it from day to day, eking out a living on his worn mat.

And then along came Peter. How amazing for Aeneas that Peter happened by when he did. Just a few words were spoken between them, and then Aeneas—who hadn't walked for eight years—stood and took a few tentative steps toward Jesus. Muscles that hadn't worked moments before suddenly worked. Joints that hadn't been used in years were now functioning properly. Tendons in need of stretching before use operated as if Aeneas had been walking every day.

So many miracles took place in Aeneas's body that day, but if you stop to think about it, God had a much bigger purpose than the healing of one man. He wanted to heal the hearts of countless men and women in the towns of Lydda and Sharon. This man's healing served as a catalyst for many to know Christ.

Don't you just love when God shows off? He can use anything He wants to draw people to Himself—a physical healing, a changed heart, a transformation in your family. . .anything. You might think that other people aren't paying attention to the things you're going through, but they are. So don't get bogged down in your personal struggles.

When Jesus comes along and says, "Pick up your mat and walk!" it's best to stand right away and brace yourself for a miracle. Don't let your doubts or fears get in the way. When Jesus moves supernaturally on your behalf, He's also hoping to touch the hearts of countless others who are looking on.

Father, I don't know whose life You are attempting to touch at the moment, but use me to help, I pray. Use my struggles, my healing, my transformations to touch the lives of those nearby. Amen.

A Turning Point

Peter replied, "Repent and be baptized, every one of you, in the name of Jesus Christ for the forgiveness of your sins. And you will receive the gift of the Holy Spirit."

ACTS 2:38 NIV

. . . .

Imagine you're on a road trip, traveling a great distance in your car. You've been behind the wheel for a couple of days now and things have gone well. Until now. You're in an unfamiliar place, feeling a little lost.

But no worries! The car is loaded with friends and family who encourage you to keep going. The GPS isn't working, at least not well, but your fellow travelers are happy to give advice on which way to go. You've come this far together already. Surely you can keep up the momentum and find your way.

You come to a fork in the road. You have to make a decision, but you're confused about which way to go. The chaos from those in the vehicle is making you a little crazy.

Now picture this story as it relates to your spiritual life. You're traveling along life's highway, going along with the crowd. Your peers and loved ones are nudging you along toward an unknown destination. Then you encounter the Lord of heaven and earth. He meets you face-to-face, and you slam on the brakes. There's no more forward movement until you know where He wants you to go. You're at a fork in the road and the decision ahead of you is critical. Either you'll follow Him. . .or you won't. This decision will affect the rest of your life.

Today, if you're at a fork in the road, turn toward Jesus. Let Him guide you from where you've been to where you need to be. His is the safest route. Down one road is death and destruction, eternal separation from God. Down the other is peace, safety, assurance of life eternal with Him and with fellow believers. Sure, turning to the right can be a little scary, especially if your friends and loved ones won't make the turn with you. But it's a choice that will (literally) turn your life around.

Father, I'll admit, I often listen to my peers instead of leaning in to hear Your still, small voice. I don't want to miss You at the next fork in the road. I commit myself to traveling with You, in this life and in the next. Amen.

Exposed

*Take no part in the worthless deeds of evil
and darkness; instead, expose them.*
EPHESIANS 5:11 NLT

. . . .

The world is full of cheaters. These clever folks cheat on tests, on their taxes, even on their spouses. They take advantage of lenient teachers and bosses and have even taken advantage of you a time or two. You're onto them and do what you can to avoid the ones with the most potential for damage, but they still manage to get their barbs in you from time to time. It's hard to shake loose of them, but you're doing your best.

The truth is most everyone is looking for a shortcut, an easier way. God doesn't want you to participate in these evil acts but rather to expose them. That's the hard part. Bravery doesn't come easily, especially when you need to shed light on someone else's sin.

When you come across someone who's cheating, you can't turn and walk the other way. Take a closer look at this verse: "Take no part in the unfruitful works of darkness, but instead expose them" (Ephesians 5:11).

So what does that look like? How do you go about exposing someone else's sin without getting caught up in the drama of it all? First, pray and ask God to shine His spotlight on the situation.

He can accomplish in an instant what you could never accomplish, even with the strongest accusations and best physical proof. His holy light can penetrate the darkness and reveal the ugly truth of what this person has done. No matter how difficult the situation, you can ask the Lord to bring the truth to light, and He will. It will happen in His time and His way, but evil will be exposed.

And remember, if there's any darkness in your heart, it will be exposed as well. Might as well get it out in the open right now, while God is doing a penetrating work. For as Ephesians 5:12 says, "It is shameful even to speak of the things that they do in secret."

It's time for full exposure.

Father, I'm keenly aware that certain individuals around me are getting away with things they shouldn't. I feel stuck and don't know what to do, so today I start by simply asking You to shine Your spotlight on them. And while You're at it, cleanse my heart too, I pray. Amen.

For Himself

Who gave himself for us to redeem us from all lawlessness and to purify for himself a people for his own possession who are zealous for good works.
TITUS 2:14

. . . .

She just couldn't figure out how to do the relationship thing. Susan tried for years—beginning with a special boyfriend in her teens. She was sure he was the one. They did everything together—parties, church functions, family events. They even worked for the same restaurant. But they eventually parted ways. He was convinced she wasn't the one.

So she tried again in college. Over a four-year period she dated three different guys, a couple of them seriously. She would get right to the "Will he pop the question?" point, when the fellow would slowly fade away.

Susan couldn't figure out what she was doing wrong. Yes, she was a little clingy. And yes, she liked his undivided attention. But she wasn't needy. . .was she?

It took a bit of counseling and a solid relationship with the man who would later become her husband before Susan figured out that she had been pushing these men away with her over-the-top neediness. Her issues stemmed from a poor relationship with her own father, going back to early childhood. Somehow she'd tried to fit these poor guys into a mold she'd created in her imagination, one that wasn't realistic.

It's strange, isn't it, that we drag our childhood experiences into adulthood. We project expectations onto people and don't even realize it. Afterward, when we're left alone (and wondering why), we're ashamed and sad, thinking no one wants to be with us. Nothing could be further from the truth. We simply need to receive the necessary healing from the past before we can move into the future.

Are you struggling with this problem in your own life? Do you project over-the-top expectations on others? Do you demand too much? Take a look at your history and try to figure out why you're doing this. God can help you bring your needs into alignment. He can heal you from the past and give you a vibrant future.

Father, thank You for showing me that I still have issues that need to be dealt with. I want to be completely healed. Show me how to let go of the pain of yesterday so that I can experience a healthy today. . .and tomorrow. Amen.

The Glory of the Lord

Now whenever the cloud lifted from the Tabernacle,
the people of Israel would set out on
their journey, following it.
EXODUS 40:36 NLT

. . . .

Ever feel overwhelmed? Confused? Lost? There's one place you can run to get the answers you need, and that's straight to God's presence. He longs to reveal Himself to you in all His glory.

If you read the story of Moses carefully, you'll see that he and Aaron regularly got alone with the Lord. They desired God's presence. And isn't it fascinating that God deliberately pulled them away from the crowd to spend time alone with Him? That's often when God tries His hardest to get our attention, when we're distracted by the crowd.

When Moses and Aaron took the time to meet with Him, God supernaturally revealed His glory. In fact, the book of Exodus reveals an amazing description of one such time:

Then the cloud covered the tent of meeting, and the
glory of the LORD filled the tabernacle. Moses could not
enter the tent of meeting because the cloud
had settled on it, and the glory of the
LORD filled the tabernacle.

In all the travels of the Israelites, whenever the cloud lifted from above the tabernacle, they would set out; but if the cloud did not lift, they did not set out—until the day it lifted. So the cloud of the LORD was over the tabernacle by day, and fire was in the cloud by night, in the sight of all the Israelites during all their travels. (Exodus 40:34–38 NIV)

What an intriguing account! They couldn't even move forward when the cloud hovered. It was almost as if the Lord was saying, "Stay here awhile. Spend time hovering in My presence, in the same way this cloud hovers over you. I long to show you My glory!"

The Lord longs to meet with us, and that means we often have to stop everything we're doing just to get alone with Him. In that beautiful, holy place, God does an amazing work of restoration and reveals Himself to us in life-changing ways.

Where are you rushing off to today? Pause. Spend some time basking in His presence and witnessing His glory.

I'm sorry I rush from here to there, Father, and miss spending time with You. I want to see Your glory! I want to bask in Your presence. Today I choose to slow down and do just that. Amen.

For His Sake

Yet if anyone suffers as a Christian, let him not be ashamed,
but let him glorify God in that name.
1 PETER 4:16

. . . .

There are Christians around the globe, even at this very moment, who are being punished for their faith. These precious people have done nothing wrong. In fact, they've done everything right. They love the Lord and are serving Him wholeheartedly. They are representing Christ well. But they have been found guilty of sharing the Gospel or speaking the name of Jesus aloud. . .and that has landed them in a difficult position, one that could even end in death.

As you ponder their fate, as you pray for their safety, their very lives, keep your eyes wide open. The Bible warns that things will get rough for believers during these last days. We need to be prepared and to stand guard against those who want to see Christianity wiped out.

The Bible warns us that perilous times will come and that people will suffer for their faith. It seems impossible that those days are upon us, but they are. Persecution is already affecting the church all over the world—at every socioeconomic level and in every country.

How do we, as a community of faith, respond?

Consider this verse: "If anyone suffers as a Christian, let him not be ashamed, but let him glorify God in that name." We respond by lifting our heads and hearts and by preparing ourselves to take a stand for what we believe.

There are those who will try to inflict shame on you once they hear you are a believer. The very name "Christian" is spoken with disdain by many, the word itself an accusation.

So what will you do in the face of persecution? Will you tuck your tail and act like you're not who you say you are, or will you bravely look the world in the eye and say, as Peter did, "I believe that Jesus is the Christ, the Son of the living God!"

Never ever be ashamed of your faith in Him. Always stand ready to give an account of what you believe, even during the hardest times.

Father, this world is a scary place at times. People try to shame me for my beliefs, but I'm not going to waver. No matter how difficult things get, I'll stand firm in my faith, Lord. Please help me. Amen.

A Vicious Cycle

"At that time I will deal with all who oppressed you. I will rescue the lame; I will gather the exiles. I will give them praise and honor in every land where they have suffered shame."
ZEPHANIAH 3:19 NIV

. . . .

Shame can be a vicious cycle, traveling down from generation to generation. It can start with one person, who then passes it on to a child, who then passes it on to another child in the next generation. It can come in subtle forms—an ugly comment over looks, poor grades, poor hygiene, or weight issues. It can come in more overt forms at the hands of a person who inflicts serious verbal and physical abuse. Those words stick like glue. They're hard to erase. The insecurities that result can grab hold of the heart and latch on for life, causing that person to treat others the same way she has been treated, though that's usually the very last thing she wants to do.

God wants to stop this cycle in your generation. He doesn't want you to play the shame game with your children. It can cease here and now. You'll spare your offspring countless years of grief if you don't join in the game. There's enough finger-pointing in the world already.

So how do you stop it? If you're a witness to abuse, intervene. Don't worry about hurting feelings. Just do what you can to protect the one being abused. Then keep a close eye on the little ones in your life to make sure they're not carrying false guilt or unnecessary shame. Cut them some slack. Don't inflict guilt over things they cannot control. And when it comes to the things they can control (food consumption, grades, friendships), tread carefully. Corrections can be made without breaking the spirit.

Think of how God fathers you. He doesn't beat you over the head or make you feel guilty when you mess up. He's right there, a loving Father, ready to sweep you into His arms and tell you how very loved you are.

That's how you break the shame game. You pour out love to those in your care.

Father, I want to put a stop to misplaced shame in my generation. I don't want my kids to struggle or to think they're failures. They're not failures. They are precious children who will impact the world for You. Help me raise them in love, I pray. Amen.

Anxiety, Be Gone!

Do not be anxious about anything, but in everything by prayer and supplication with thanksgiving let your requests be made known to God. And the peace of God, which surpasses all understanding, will guard your hearts and your minds in Christ Jesus.

PHILIPPIANS 4:6–7

. . . .

Look at any photograph or painting of President Abraham Lincoln and you will see a somber-faced man. If you didn't know any better, you might say, "That fellow looks a little sour." He carried a lot of weight on his shoulders, to be sure. If you study his life, you will learn that he went through major tragedies in his childhood. As a youngster, he lost his mother. Then, while still in his teens, his precious older sister passed away. After he married, he and his wife had twelve children, ten of whom passed away during childhood. (Can you even imagine?)

Yes, Lincoln had his fair share of losses. And he struggled with feelings of inadequacy as well, in part due to his poor upbringing. No doubt, anxiety was his close companion at times.

Somehow Lincoln managed to overcome all of this and move forward. In fact, he's known as one of the most important political figures in American history. If he had allowed the pain or anguish of his past to stop him in his tracks, the course of a nation might have been changed forever.

Your life is meant to effect change as well. If you allow yourself to get bogged down in the mire of yesterday, if you feel shame over where you've come from or the obstacles you've faced, you won't be as effective. It's time to think about your possibilities. . . today. Like Lincoln, you can overcome and make a difference in the lives of those around you. Let go of those anxieties and let your requests be made known to God. He's listening, and He cares.

Father, I've faced hardships. I've been through low places.
And I'm not necessarily the best candidate to reach
others. But You've chosen me, Lord, to make a difference.
So I let go of any inadequacies and anxieties
and say, "Use me, Lord!" Amen.

The Assurance of Things Hoped For

Now faith is confidence in what we hope for and assurance about what we do not see. This is what the ancients were commended for. By faith we understand that the universe was formed at God's command, so that what is seen was not made out of what was visible.

HEBREWS 11:1–3 NIV

. . . .

Remember when you were a child, how you waited with anticipation for Christmas morning? In fact, you could barely sleep the night before. The weeks leading up to the big day were riddled with questions: "What will I find under the tree?" "Will I really get that Radio Flyer wagon I've been wanting?" "Will Mom like that necklace I made her?" "Will Dad like the tools we bought him?" "What kind of pies will Grandma make for Christmas dinner?" "Are we going to watch Christmas movies this year?"

Even then, as a small child, you had faith to believe that something wonderful was about to occur. Regardless of your economic status, you felt sure something terrific would be waiting for you on Christmas morning. You could count on it because you knew the adults in your world would make it happen. And even if the Christmases prior had been sparse, you still hoped against hope that this year would be different. The TV commercials told you it would. The store windows gave you hope with their glittering displays. You had much to look forward to, and nothing would dampen your spirit.

Faith is much the same. It gives us the courage to believe for great things, even when we can't yet see them with our eyes. That sense of anticipation you felt as a child? It's back once more, bubbling up inside of you as you look forward to the great things God has in store for you. In fact, you can hardly wait. God is trustworthy, even more so than your parents were.

God wants us to have childlike faith, to believe Him for great things. He wants you to be sure of the things you're hoping for and willing to "see" the things you can't yet see with your eyes. What are you anticipating today? What gets you excited? Trust God in all things, big and small, and watch Him move on your behalf.

I'm believing for big things, Lord! Thank You for increasing my faith. I wait with anticipation, Father. Amen.

Rescued from Trials

The Lord knows how to rescue the godly from trials,
and to keep the unrighteous under punishment
until the day of judgment.
2 PETER 2:9

Deena found it embarrassing, truth be told. An introvert since childhood, she certainly wasn't looking for attention. But the tragedies she'd suffered over the past few years put her squarely in the center of attention among her family and friends. First cancer, now the death of her husband? It was hard enough to handle on her own, but the over-the-top attention from friends and church members was almost too much to handle. She couldn't very well say, "Please go away. I'm not keen on people hanging around." But that's what she felt like saying at times.

Deena was embarrassed that she felt the way she did. What was wrong with her, anyway? Most of her friends would want—even desire—close companionship after such a rough season. Why was she so different from everyone? Why did she want to curl up on the sofa with a good book and ask the world to go away and leave her alone?

Maybe you connect with Deena's feelings. Maybe you're a bit introverted too. Going through a trauma is hard enough, but dealing with the onslaught of extra attention is overwhelming.

You don't want to be rude, but you're not used to it. It exhausts you. You just want to be left alone.

These feelings leave you guilt-ridden, but what can you do? God designed you as an introvert, after all. It's hard to fight who you are, especially now, when your resistance is down.

Perhaps this is the time to confide in a good friend—someone who can share with the others—that you need a bit of space. Believe it or not, people really will understand. Take whatever time you need to heal, to grieve, to be in God's presence. Then when you're ready, go out to lunch with a friend. Or two. Do it on your terms and in a way that makes you feel comfortable. And don't feel guilty about it. We all grieve differently, after all.

Father, I know that others would probably want to be surrounded by people, but it's hard for me. Show me how to accept the love of my friends without feeling like I'm suffocating. More than anything, I need time with You, Lord. Amen.

Spreading the Gospel

Therefore God exalted him to the highest place and gave him the name that is above every name, that at the name of Jesus every knee should bow, in heaven and on earth and under the earth, and every tongue acknowledge that Jesus Christ is Lord, to the glory of God the Father.

PHILIPPIANS 2:9–11 NIV

In 1858 the Lord began to move across the city of Philadelphia, Pennsylvania. One of the participating ministers was a bold, unwavering young Episcopalian by the name of Dudley Tyng. Not only was this twenty-nine-year-old minister busy pastoring his own congregation, but he also started daily noon services at the YMCA in downtown Philadelphia.

Huge crowds came to hear Dudley speak. On a particular Tuesday over five thousand men gathered to hear him preach on the topic of serving the Lord. One-fifth of the men (over one thousand of them) committed their hearts to the Lord that amazing day.

Here's the awesome part: Dudley wasn't thinking about trying to build a church or add numbers to his congregation. He was genuinely interested in saving souls, as we should be.

So where do you stand on winning people to the Lord? Is it your passion or something you only think of when you come face-to-face with people who don't know Him? No need to feel bad if you've fallen down in this area. There's still plenty of time to get back up again. Winning people to Christ should be a priority; God has called you to make an impact in your world.

Father, I want to do my part. Like Dudley Tyng, I want to make a difference in my generation. I won't waste any time with regrets over years wasted. Show me how I can get to work right here, right now. Amen.

The Call of God

"Therefore go and make disciples of all nations, baptizing them in the name of the Father and of the Son and of the Holy Spirit, and teaching them to obey everything I have commanded you. And surely I am with you always, to the very end of the age."

MATTHEW 28:19–20 NIV

. . . .

These powerful words, straight from the lips of our Savior, have propelled thousands of people onto the mission field. Of course, not everyone has a calling to go to the deepest, darkest jungles of Africa to preach the Gospel. But many do, and they are faced with the ultimate challenge—to respond to the call or to stay inside their comfort zone.

One man who had to struggle with that call was David Livingstone. When he applied to the London Missionary Society, this Scottish missionary and abolitionist was assigned to South Africa. To put this prospect in perspective, this was before the days of highways and GPS.

Livingstone stepped out in faith and accepted the path before him, but he faced multiple hardships and sorrows along the way, including illness and the death of his wife.

Still, David's obedience stands as a testimony to us all. He served with humility and placed his own desires and wishes in second place to the call on his life. His desire to see souls enter the kingdom of God far surpassed any personal wants and wishes. His objective—to open a missionary road into the interior of Africa—was key so that unreached people groups could hear the Gospel.

Maybe you have struggled with the call of God on your life. You feel Him tugging, but you're too overwhelmed or insecure to answer. So you simply stay put and try to drown out His still, small voice.

Today, God wants you to tune in to what He's saying. He wants to increase your confidence and remind you that He will give you all you need to make it from point A to point B. You can trust Him to guide you as you step out in faith.

Confidence has a great reward, as Hebrews 10:35 says. If you don't believe it, ask David Livingstone when you see him in heaven.

Lord, I know You've placed a call on my life. I sense it deeply at times. Give me the courage and the guidance to step out when the timing is right. I want to do great things for You, Father. Amen.

Confounded

But God chose what is foolish in the world to shame the wise; God chose what is weak in the world to shame the strong; God chose what is low and despised in the world, even things that are not, to bring to nothing things that are, so that no human being might boast in the presence of God. And because of him you are in Christ Jesus, who became to us wisdom from God, righteousness and sanctification and redemption.

1 CORINTHIANS 1:27–30

. . . .

The world is full of people who've had the benefit of higher education. They are book smart and often happy to share their expertise with you. In fact, many of them are very proud of their diplomas and the letters behind their names. And why not? They attended college for years, after all! So you bear with them as they get puffed up with pride telling you about their various degrees. You marvel when you're in their presence and even feel a little intimidated when you dare to compare your knowledge level with theirs.

Then you spend time with them and realize they don't know as much as they say they know. You see right through the "smarts" to the areas of their lives that are lacking. Isn't it funny that some of these same people don't seem to have a lot of common sense? Instead of using their knowledge to live safe, godly lives, they veer away from God altogether. What they have in knowledge they lack in wisdom.

By the same token, certain people have very little education but are some of the wisest people you know. They seem to be in tune with the Holy Spirit at all times. This wisdom doesn't come from books or college professors or assignments. It's straight from heaven.

God has always used the foolish things of this world to confound the wise. (Don't believe it? Listen to a seven-year-old philosophize about the world!) We have to be willing to open our hearts and our ears so that we can learn from others, even those we least suspect.

Who are you learning from today? Who is learning from you?

Father, I'll admit, I've placed a lot of emphasis on knowledge. Sometimes I forget that wisdom is just as important, if not more so. I don't want to be book smart but life foolish. Use whoever (or whatever) You choose to teach me, Lord. I am Your ready student. Amen.

Power in Numbers

Therefore, confess your sins to one another and pray for one another, that you may be healed. The prayer of a righteous person has great power as it is working.

JAMES 5:16

Carol had a great circle of friends. They were fairly open with each other about the challenges they faced in life. At least, her friends were. Carol had a harder time sharing the stuff she was going through. She found herself torn between not wanting to bother the other women and not wanting to crack the facade that everything in her life was hunky-dory. She'd done a great job of convincing people her world was pretty perfect, after all. No point in destroying her image with the truth.

From the time she was a child, Carol was taught to keep her feelings inside, to internalize even the deepest agonies. So every regret, every shameful situation, every pain got tucked away. Her friends and loved ones would say, "That Carol! She's always smiling. She's sure got her act together." Many wanted to be like her, since she clearly lived an ideal life. But on the inside, Carol continued to struggle. . .all the while with a broad smile on her face, of course, lest the facade crack.

Can you relate to Carol? Do you try to put forth the image that everything in your world is perfect when it's really not? Are you afraid to open up, even to those you're closest to? Sure, you want to look like you're in terrific shape. Anything less and you might crack open like an overboiled egg.

It's pointless to pretend. Suppression isn't healthy, even if your motivation is to spare those you love from unnecessary drama. It's time to come clean, to let others know what you're really dealing with. The Bible says that we are to confess our sins to one another and pray for one another. There's great healing in sharing. So no more hiding. No more facades. Let others see the real you. They can handle it. And God will honor your willingness to come clean. In fact, He will probably use your friends to help you heal.

Father, it's easier to hide sometimes. I don't like to air my dirty laundry or expose my secrets. But You're calling me to open up and share. I want to come clean so that I can fully heal. Help me, I pray. Amen.

The Right to Become Children

But to all who believed him and accepted him,
he gave the right to become children of God.
JOHN 1:12 NLT

. . . .

Marianna had a hard time fitting in. She struggled with the way she looked and didn't feel as pretty as other women. She was socially awkward and struggled to make conversation in a large group, which made things even harder. So she kept to herself a lot. It was just easier that way.

She felt embarrassed and ashamed of herself for not trying harder, but what would be the point? What if she put herself out there only to be ridiculed or ostracized? Others didn't gravitate toward her, anyway. They'd never know the difference if she slipped out of the party or event before anyone else. In fact, most probably didn't even notice she'd arrived in the first place.

Here's a difficult truth: much of Marianna's problem was in her thought life. She hadn't really given people a chance. How could she know for sure they would reject her if she didn't put herself out there? It's difficult when you've been rejected in the past, but God can give you the courage to try again, if you just ask Him to.

Maybe you can relate. It's easier to just say no to invitations. It's less traumatizing to stay home and eat ice cream and watch movies by yourself, or to browse social media instead of talking to people in person. But God designed you to live in community. He wants to surround you with people who can share your load and pray for you when you're in need. That means you'll have to actually get out and be among people, even if it's hard. The longer you stay away, the harder it will be.

Today, give your fears and concerns to the Lord. If you're worried that people will see your imperfections, stop stressing! People will love you even more if you open up and share your flaws with them.

So relax. Be yourself. Then watch God move you into deep and authentic relationships.

It's going to take courage, Father, but I'm ready to put myself out there. I need friends. I need confidantes. I'm tired of withdrawing from the crowd, of being alone. I'll be vulnerable, Lord. I'll let people see the real me. Help me as I open up, I pray. Amen.

God Will Hear

*But as for me, I will look to the LORD; I will wait for
the God of my salvation; my God will hear me.*
MICAH 7:7

. . . .

"What is wrong with me?" Lisa asked herself as she drove home
from the party. Everything about the evening had been off. She
couldn't seem to settle down and just be herself. She'd spent
the whole evening trying to entertain people—telling stories,
making them laugh, working overtime to impress them with the
food she'd brought.

All of it was exhausting. And she hadn't intended any of that.
In her mind's eye, the whole event was a lovely opportunity to
hang out with friends and visit, not try to sell herself. Why had she
felt compelled to do that, anyway? Was she not getting enough
attention? Did she feel left out in some way?

Maybe you've been in Lisa's shoes. You were struggling to
fit in, so you worked overtime to impress your peers. Your efforts
were over the top, not because it suited you to work so hard, but
because you thought they might find some value in you if you
impressed them.

Only, they didn't seem overly impressed. In fact, most didn't
even seem to notice at all. So you felt crushed. Next time you'd do
better. You'd try harder. You'd come up with some way to feel noticed.

If any of this is ringing a bell, perhaps it's time to ask the Lord what's really missing in your life. God never intended for you to have to work so hard to maintain friendships. And He never wanted you to feel as if you weren't worthy of others' love. In fact, God's greatest desire is for you to accept the notion that your value is found in Him, not in your actions.

Deep breath. Maybe you need to unpack your emotions a bit, to get the answer to the "why?" question. Once you know why you're feeling the need to impress others, you'll be better equipped to fix the problem. In the meantime, allow God to show you that you don't need to jump through any hoops to impress Him. He's madly in love with you already.

Father, thank You for the reminder that I don't need to impress You. And I don't need to impress others either. Help me unpack my reasons for feeling the way I do. Do I need to be needed? Do I need to feel wanted? Give me Your perspective, then help me move forward in a way that honors You. Amen.

Never Again

"Then you will know that I am in Israel, that I am the
LORD your God, and that there is no other;
never again will my people be shamed."
JOEL 2:27 NIV

. . . .

When you think of the words *never again*, what comes to mind? Maybe you're in a relationship with someone who lies. A lot. He's said, "I won't lie again, I promise. Never again." But you know you can't trust him. You've made that mistake in the past, and you won't be doing it again.

Or maybe you're on a diet. You've sworn off sodas. You've told yourself, "Never again. I won't drink my favorite soda. . .ever." Only, you break the promise to yourself. And once that promise is broken, once you've had that first sip, it's hard to turn back. And now you're ashamed of yourself because you did something you said you wouldn't do. You messed up.

Perhaps you've promised your child a trip to an amusement park over spring break. Only, the holiday is approaching and you haven't set aside enough money. You're going to have to let your child down. . .again. And you're heartbroken because, once again, you didn't follow through.

Take a look at this scripture. God has promised that you will never again be shamed. He's a good, good Father. He won't speak words of shame over you no matter what you do.

God is trustworthy. He's not a liar. If He says you'll never again be put to shame, you can believe it. He will lift you above any reproach or shame and set you free forevermore. Any soul ties to shame (or to others who've participated in your actions) can and will be broken for good. But it will require effort on your part: you have to separate yourself from yesterday and make a decision to step into today.

What teensy-tiny part of your heart wants to stay linked to shame? Why? Picture yourself with a pair of scissors, snipping away that last little thread so that you can step away permanently. Once you're free, you will be free indeed.

Lord, I hadn't considered soul ties until now. Who—or what—
am I linked to? What final thread do I need to cut in order
to be fully set free? Please help me with those scissors,
Lord. I'm ready to be done with the past,
but I will need Your help. Amen.

A Blameless Walk

LORD, who may dwell in your sacred tent? Who may live on
your holy mountain? The one whose walk is blameless,
who does what is righteous, who speaks
the truth from their heart.
PSALM 15:1–2 NIV

You've likely heard the expression "We're all products of our environment." To a certain extent this is true, but there are times when that phrase can be a bit of a cop-out or an excuse not to change. We learn from our parents how to respond to life's circumstances, good and bad. Gleaning from Mom and Dad, we become either actors (acting responsibly) or reactors (knee-jerking to every little thing).

If you grew up in a home where everyone reacted (or overreacted), perhaps you learned to do the same quite naturally. You didn't set out to be rude or impulsive. It just happened over time without your awareness. Maybe you don't take the time to think things through before jumping to conclusions because that's what you were taught to do. Instead, you make big deals out of small ones. You blow things out of proportion.

This extreme response to life's challenges can lead to drama, not just for yourself but for others as well. Impulsive reactions can cause your temper to flare and your blood pressure to rise and can put you at greater risk for heart problems, not to mention tension headaches.

It's not too late. No matter how you grew up, you can change the way you react to challenges. You can learn to think carefully before you speak or act. You can become more subdued, more thoughtful.

So how do you begin? Acknowledge the situation. Put words to it: "I'm a reactor, and I need to change." You can get past the shame brought on by exaggerated responses if you learn to take a deep breath and think before you have any sort of reaction, verbal or physical.

Most of all, you can ask the Holy Spirit—who resides inside of you if you're a believer—to take control of your emotions. He longs to do that even now.

Father, I want to be an actor, behaving responsibly, not a reactor. It's exhausting to blow up at every little thing. And I always end up embarrassed and ashamed after I've made a fool of myself. Help me to temper my responses and to represent You well. I want to learn from You how to respond to others. Help me, I pray. Amen.

Hope in God

Why am I discouraged? Why is my heart so sad?
I will put my hope in God! I will praise him
again—my Savior and my God!
Psalm 42:11 NLT

. . . .

Nancy was one of those women who always seemed to be down in the dumps. She wasn't clinically depressed or going through a particularly challenging season. Life wasn't working against her. She had a good job, a sweet husband, a nice home. She was just. . .sullen. Sour. Unhappy. And she tended to bring down the mood of the whole room whenever she attended an event, though she might have been surprised to hear people say that about her.

She couldn't help but complain—about every ache and pain, everything anyone had ever done to hurt or offend her. She grumbled about everything—from the weather to her workload. If you were to ask her how she felt about being set free from these feelings, she would probably shrug. Because at the core of her being, she enjoyed the attention and had adapted to being down in the dumps. It suited her. Why change?

Does Nancy's story strike a chord? Can you relate? Would people say that you're sullen. . .or upbeat? It might suit your personality to be down more than up, but perpetual sullenness can affect your walk with the Lord and with others if you don't take the time to deal with it. And remember, you're a reflection of Christ to all you come in contact with. When they begin to see you as grumpy or cross, they wonder if the God you serve might be the same way. That's not the image you mean to portray.

So smile! Let go of that attitude. Begin to let the love of Christ shine through you. He can take that sour expression and replace it with joy—not the manufactured kind, but the real deal. And, honestly? Wouldn't you rather be genuinely joyful than to experience attention based on your sullenness? God can turn your situation (and your responses) around if you let Him.

Lord, I don't want to be known as a grump. Sometimes I feel like I've let my negative emotions and reactions rule the day. Help me overcome this tendency, Father. There are so many wonderful ways to reflect You. May I be the best possible witness to others, I pray. Amen.

The Righteousness of God

*For our sake he made him to be sin who knew no sin,
so that in him we might become the righteousness of God.*
2 Corinthians 5:21

· ·

Carrie had a hard time forgiving others. She didn't hold grudges on a conscious level, of course. In fact, if you asked her about it, she would claim that she'd let go of all the grudges ages ago and that she had forgiven those who had hurt her. But every time her ex-husband's name came up in conversation, she would cringe. . .then dive into a litany of complaints about him. She did the same with her ex-mother-in-law, a woman she still despised. And, of course, that woman at work who'd done her wrong. And the neighbor who turned her in to the homeowners association for not taking down her Christmas lights. Her stories were memorized and passionate. She could tell them with style and leave an audience spellbound. And yet, not once did it occur to her that she hadn't fully forgiven those she was talking about.

Whether she wanted to admit it or not, Carrie had a hard time letting go. Period. She even found it difficult to forgive herself for mistakes she'd made in the past. Only when a good friend took the time to sit with her and share her thoughts on all of this did Carrie see that these grudges, this unforgiveness, were affecting her current relationships and her relationship with the Lord.

Maybe you can relate. Maybe there are a few people in your past you've had a hard time forgiving. You're not consciously carrying a grudge, but when someone mentions that name, your blood curdles.

Here's the truth: God wants us to let go of grudges, not just because they hurt the people we're angry with, but because they affect us—physically, emotionally, and psychologically. And remember, the Bible says that we're to forgive others as God forgives us. How can He forgive us if we refuse to let go of grudges?

It's time to release those who've hurt you. Time to make a list and do business with the Lord. You'll feel so good once this process is over.

Father, today I acknowledge that I've held a few grudges.
There are people whose names have caused me to cringe.
I release them back to You, and I offer forgiveness.
Help me to step beyond what I'm feeling to
the fullness of forgiveness in You. Amen.

Sinless but Scorned

Again and again they struck him on the head with a staff and spit on him. Falling on their knees, they paid homage to him.
MARK 15:19 NIV

It's sad to think that certain ethnic groups or people groups are facing persecution even now. They are tormented and tortured by other people groups because they are different—politically, socially, economically. Some are attacked because they have different religious beliefs or customs. Many have been made to feel ashamed, even by people in their own groups, because they look different or have different loyalties.

While most Christians enjoy comfortable lives and attend their church service of choice without fear, many people across the planet are being persecuted for their faith in Christ. Even now, many live in terror of being martyred, or at the very least ridiculed and tortured. They are made to feel ashamed for not believing in the more popular gods of their nations. The pressure to bow down to false gods is overwhelming at times, but faithful followers of Jesus Christ refuse to give in. They stand firm, even in the face of death, offering their very lives in service to their King. Is there any higher honor? Any greater crown?

Jesus can relate to these precious believers. He knows what it feels like to be despised and rejected, even by His own people.

He understands the pain of torture and abuse at the hands of people who should have accepted Him. More than anything, He knows what it's like to remain faithful and yet be tormented by those who are unfaithful.

Today, take the time to pray for those around the world who are being forced to suffer shame and abuse. They have a heavy cross to bear. You can lighten their load, at least on some level, by remembering them in prayer. And do what you can to help. Give to organizations that protect the innocent. And never take for granted the freedoms that you have to share the Gospel.

Father, my eyes are wide open. I want to do what I can to help my fellow believers. I lift them up in prayer today. Guard and protect them, I pray. Show me what I can do to help. And help me to stand firm in my faith, never bowing to the pressures around me, even when times get tough. Amen.

The Road to Repentance

The Lord is not slow to fulfill his promise as some count slowness, but is patient toward you, not wishing that any should perish, but that all should reach repentance.
2 PETER 3:9

· ·

If you've parented a small child, you know what it's like to give second chances. And third. And fourth. And if you've navigated the world of parenting a teen, you come to understand that starting over—again and again and again—can become a lifestyle. We all need fresh starts from time to time.

God is just like that hopeful parent. He really wishes that His kiddo (you) would learn the lesson the first time around. But He's also patient and forgiving, ready to offer additional opportunities when you mess up. And you will mess up. It's a given. But He never gives up on you, no matter how far you stray.

Why is God so patient? He longs for all to come to know Him and to spend eternity with Him. Ponder that for a second. If you knew that your child would face eternal separation from you, wouldn't you wait as long as it took for him to make things right? Of course you would. You'd cross mountains to bring that loved one back home. You would do whatever it took. That's how love operates.

No parent wants to lose a child or watch one pull away from

a family of faith. Think of the prodigal son, racing from the nest, eager to squander his inheritance. Even after he made a spectacle of himself, his father stood with arms wide open, ready to welcome him home. Can you imagine the shame the son must have felt as he returned home with his tail tucked between his legs? And yet his dad was so excited to see him that he threw down the welcome mat and hosted the party of the decade. That's how love operates. It gives and gives and then gives some more.

God isn't interested in rubbing your nose in your mistakes. He doesn't want you to stay long in that "tail tucked between the legs" posture. He wants to watch you, His precious child, return home for good.

Father, I've felt like a prodigal at times. I've squandered time, money, opportunities. But You're so gracious and welcoming. I've experienced Your open arms, ushering me back home again. I'm so grateful for Your love, Lord. Amen.

God Is True

He bears witness to what he has seen and heard, yet no one receives his testimony. Whoever receives his testimony sets his seal to this, that God is true.
John 3:32–33

. . . .

God is true.

No matter what you've been told about Him, no matter what the media or political leaders might try to sway you to believe, God is true. In fact, He's the only real truth in the world.

People will fail you. Political parties will fail you. Knowledge will fail you. Romance will fail you. Moving up the corporate ladder will fail you.

But God will never fail you because He is truth.

When you've settled that issue in your heart, it's easy to put your trust in Him. And nothing is more comforting than being able to trust. You're completely relaxed when you're in trust mode.

Knowing that God will keep His word should bring peace and comfort to your heart. According to 1 Peter 1:25 (NLT), "The word of the Lord remains forever." It's reliable, enduring, eternal. Nothing about God ever changes.

Think about that for a moment. You change from second to second. Your body changes, your mind changes, your thoughts change, even your habits and preferences change. Your friends change, you change your clothes, your income changes. You change schools, homes, neighborhoods, and cities. Everything around is in a constant state of flux—from the ticking clock to the balance in your checking account to the blood coursing through your veins even now. Nothing remains still, even for a moment.

But God. . .He never changes. He's true—yesterday, today, and tomorrow. Even if we are completely unfaithful to the Lord, He will never be unfaithful to us.

What a gracious, steady, truthful God we serve. He's our unmovable rock, and we're exceedingly blessed to be His children.

Father, I'm so grateful for Your eternal truth. You're the same God who created everything. Nothing about You has changed. I've settled the issue in my heart. You're a God of Your word, true from eternity to eternity. Oh, how I love You, Lord. How I trust You! Amen.

Forever

The LORD knows the days of the blameless, and their heritage will remain forever; they are not put to shame in evil times; in the days of famine they have abundance.
PSALM 37:18–19

. . . .

When you think about the word *legacy*, what comes to mind? Do you think of the physical inheritance you'll one day leave your children and grandchildren—the home, car, money, or other material possessions that will be passed down after you're gone? Or do you think of your rich spiritual heritage, which you hope will travel from generation to generation long beyond your time on planet Earth?

We all hope that our offspring will love and serve Christ. It's foremost in our minds, especially during these last days when proclaiming our faith is becoming harder and harder. Perhaps you can imagine what your grandchildren and their grandchildren will be like, how they all will serve Christ, in spite of any obstacles. You can picture them standing tall during seasons of oppression.

As you ponder your heritage, as you think about what you'll pass down, give this verse from Psalms another glance. The Lord knows your days. He knew the days of your parents and grandparents as well. He knows how long you'll live and what will happen to your children after you're gone. And He's already thinking about the heritage you'll leave behind, even while you're still here.

Isn't it remarkable to think that God will always take care of your family? Even in times of famine (financial, spiritual, emotional, or even physical), He will be right there, taking care of everything. He'll make sure your loved ones are well taken care of. It's on Him, not you.

Your heritage will remain forever. You can look forward to seeing your loved ones again in heaven. That family legacy, which began with the very first member who accepted Christ, is now developing into a long chain of people who adore you and adore Him. What a wonderful way to impact the world, one generation at a time.

Lord, I'm so grateful for my legacy. I'm grateful for those who came before me and those who are coming after. I know that You know the number of our days, and I'm fully trusting You with my future. I can count on You to keep this legacy going long after I've crossed over into eternity with You. Praise You, Lord! Amen.

Not Your Own Doing

For by grace you have been saved through faith.
And this is not your own doing; it is the gift of God,
not a result of works, so that no one may boast.
EPHESIANS 2:8–9

. . . .

It's not your own doing.

Think about those words for a minute. Likely, you depend on yourself for pretty much everything. If there's a task that needs to be done, you do it. If there are kids to be fed, you feed them. If there's a mortgage to be paid, you get a job, earn the money, and pay it. If the car needs to be washed, you wash it (or drive through the car wash).

Isn't it refreshing to know that there's one area of your life where Someone else takes the reins? What you couldn't do for yourself, Christ did on the cross. He took your sin, once and for all, and rid you of it. He gave you a second chance at life and an opportunity to spend all of eternity with Him. And He did all of that without your help.

So the next time you start to feel overwhelmed or ashamed, remember. . .the work is complete. To revisit your shame is to tell Jesus that what He did wasn't enough.

It *was* enough, it *is* enough, and it *will continue to be* enough, no matter how many times you trip up. Because, again, it's not dependent on you. (Whew! What a relief!)

You will trip up, you know. And you need to stop beating yourself up over it. When you fall, stand back up again, brush yourself off, and accept the grace and mercy of a Savior who adores you. Don't tell Him how to do His job. Just trust that He's already completed the work that needed to be done on your behalf.

It's not up to you.

Let those words sink in.

It's not up to you.

Father, I'm so glad I'm not responsible for my own salvation.
You had the plan. You acted on it. You fulfilled all that needed
to be fulfilled on Calvary. All I ever had to do was accept
the work of Christ on the cross and apply it to my life.
I'm so grateful You have set me free from the law of sin and
death and have shown me how to live a shame-free life.
I praise You, Lord, for the free gift of salvation. Amen.

Discover More Spiritual
Refreshment for Your Soul with...

Untroubled: Devotions and Prayers
for Finding Calm in a Chaotic World

Whether you worry about your children, your work,
your relationships, the troubles of the world,
or something more, God is ever present and faithful
to give you the peace you need to be *Untroubled*.
Featuring more than 120 devotional readings plus
inspiring prayers and scripture selections, this delightful
devotional will encourage you to spend purposeful,
one-on-one time with your loving heavenly Creator.

Hardcover / 978-1-68322-946-9 / $12.99